Adlerian Group Counseling and Therapy
Step-by-Step

Adlerian Group Counseling *and* Therapy *Step-by-Step*

Manford A. Sonstegard
James Robert Bitter
with Peggy Pelonis

Routledge
Taylor & Francis Group
LONDON AND NEW YORK

Cover photo: © Ken Whitmore
Cover design: Elise Weinger

First published 2004 by
Brunner-Routledge

Published 2014 by
Routledge
711 Third Avenue,
New York, NY 10017

Published in Great Britain by
Routledge
2 Park Square, Milton Park,
Abingdon, Oxfordshihe OX14 4RN

First issued in paperback 2014

Routledge is an imprint of the Taylor and Francis Group, an informa business

Copyright © 2004 by Taylor & Francis Books, Inc.

All rights reserved. No part of this book may be reprinted or reproduced or utilized in any form or by any electronic, mechanical, or other means, now know or hereafter invented, including photocopying and recording, or in any information storage or retrieval system, without permission in writing from the publishers.

Library of Congress Cataloging-in-Publication Data

Sonstegard, Manford A.
  Adlerian group counseling & therapy : step-by-step / Manford A. Sonstegard and James Robert Bitter, with Peggy Pelonis ; foreword by Gerald Corey.
    p. ; cm.
Includes bibliographical references and index.
    ISBN 978-0-415-94820-3 (hardback : alk. paper)
  1. Group psychotherapy. 2. Group counseling. 3. Adlerian psychology.
    [DNLM: 1. Psychotherapy, Group—methods. WM 430 S698a 2004] I. Title: Adlerian group counseling and therapy. II. Bitter, James Robert.
III. Pelonis, Peggy. IV. Title.
  RC488.S628 2004
  616.89'152—dc22   2003018213

ISBN 978-0-415-94820-3 (hbk)
ISBN 978-1-138-87158-8 (pbk)

Dedications

Manford A. Sonstegard
To my wife and partner, Rita Sonstegard

James Robert Bitter
To my life partner Lynn Williams and to our children Alison and Nora

Contents

Foreword by Gerald Corey — *ix*

Acknowledgments — *xiii*

Manford A. Sonstegard: The Man and His Therapy
An Introduction by James Robert Bitter — *xv*

Part I: The Process and Practice of Adlerian Group Counseling and Therapy

Chapter 1. A Rationale for Adlerian Group Work — 3

Chapter 2. Adlerian Group Counseling and Therapy: Step by Step — 17

Part II: Theoretical Foundations

Chapter 3. Theory, Process, and Structure in Adlerian Group Work — 59

Chapter 4. The Practice of Adlerian Group Counseling and Therapy — 95

Chapter 5. Counseling Children in Groups — 135

Chapter 6. The Education and Training of Group Specialists — 161
By James Robert Bitter, Peggy Pelonis, and Manford A. Sonstegard

Authors' Notes — 185

Indexes — 187

Foreword

Adlerian Group Counseling & Therapy: Step by Step is a book you will want to read if you are interested in the theory and practice of group counseling. In this book, Drs. Manford Sonstegard and Jim Bitter bring to life group counseling from an Adlerian perspective. They clearly describe the process and practice of Adlerian group therapy through commentaries and transcribed interactions of their group process. They also concisely describe key concepts of Adlerian theory that can be applied to Adlerian groups as well as to a host of other groups that rest on different theoretical foundations.

Alfred Adler made significant contributions to contemporary therapeutic practice of both individual and group counseling and psychotherapy. Adler was the first psychiatrist to use group methods in a systematic way in child guidance centers in the 1920s in Vienna. Building on Adler's work, Rudolf Dreikurs did a great deal to translate and develop Adlerian principles into the practice of group counseling and group therapy in both private and public settings. Adlerian interventions have been widely applied to diverse client populations, with all ages, and in many different settings—but especially in schools.

Adler's contributions to the development of group counseling have far-reaching implications to the development of many other therapeutic models. In many ways, Adler can be considered a significant pioneer in the field of group counseling, influencing models based on dynamics, cognitions, emotional response, and existential meaning. A number of theories in the cognitive-behavioral camp clearly have some roots in Adlerian principles and contributions, including rational-emotive-behavior therapy and cognitive therapy. Further, many of Adler's ideas have been incorporated in the writing and theories of Rollo May, Viktor Frankl, and Abraham Maslow. Both Frankl and May considered Adler to be a forerunner of the existential movement, because Adler believed that human beings were free to choose and were entirely responsible for what they make of themselves. This view also places Adler at the center of the subjective approach to psychology, an approach that focuses on the internal determinants of behavior: values, beliefs, attitudes, goals, interests, personal meaning, perceptions of reality, and striving toward self-actualization. All of these concepts have important implications for the practice of group counseling and therapy.

Adlerian Group Counseling & Therapy: Step by Step represents a distillation of some of the most significant ideas of Alfred Adler and Rudolf Dreikurs as applied to group work. Drs. Sonstegard and Bitter provide a compelling rationale for the practice of group work. These authors illustrate the development of a group from the formation to the final stage, giving readers a clear picture of what is important to accomplish at each stage of a group. This book also addresses many practical dimensions of Adlerian group process, including the importance of forming a group relationship; how to create a democratic and accepting climate in a group; ways group counselors can conduct a psychological assessment of each of the members of a group; approaches to increasing awareness and insight on the part of members; techniques aimed at helping members translate their insights into actions; and methods of reorientation and reeducation through encouragement and building on the personal strengths discovered within the group experience. The authors describe and use an active style of group leadership that offers a structure to assist group members in getting the most from a counseling group. Although the approach they describe can be considered directive at times, Adlerians are highly respectful of the group members and their capacities to play an active part in the growth experiences inherent in group process. Adlerian group counseling is a collaborative approach that can get results and lead to empowerment of the members.

I found the chapter on the theory and practice of Adlerian group counseling particularly valuable in serving as a review of key concepts and specific group techniques. Some of the concepts concisely described include holism, teleological orientation, community feeling and its social interest, lifestyle and its assessment, and the encouragement process, to name a few. Drs. Sonstegard and Bitter highlight a number of interventions that can be usefully applied to many different kinds of groups with diverse client populations. A few of the techniques that I found particularly useful are interpretation, uses of "The Question," lifestyle assessment, early recollections, and challenging basic beliefs. Although the techniques may be of interest to many readers, it is my belief that the Adlerian philosophy underlying group practice is what will be most valuable to readers. Personally, I have incorporated much of an Adlerian philosophy into my practice of group work and find that this approach gives me a strong foundation as well as a great deal of freedom. Because of its breadth, the model is also able to utilize techniques drawn from other theoretical models. Readers of *Adlerian Counseling & Therapy: Step by Step* will find the book meaningful, regardless of their level of experience in facilitating groups.

—Gerald Corey, EdD
Professor Emeritus, Human Services
California State University at Fullerton

Acknowledgments

We have many people to acknowledge, starting with those who taught us and made us their colleagues: Rudolf and Tee Dreikurs, Heinz and Rowena Ansbacher, Eva Dreikurs Ferguson, Oscar and Mary Christensen, and Robert L. Powers and Jane Griffith. We are also indebted to Jon Carlson and Guy Manaster for their many years of editing the *Journal of Individual Psychology*, a primary source for our work; and to the skills and scholarship of Marion Balla, Carolyn Zoe Crowder, Clair Hawes, Harold Mosak, Gerald Mozdzierz, Bill Nicoll, Angela Roberts, Robert Sherman, Bernard Shulman, Don Smart, Kirsten Sonstegard, and Len Sperry. We also want to acknowledge our students who have honored us with their work: Judy Bradford, Kathie Hoffman, Heidi Matson, Karen O'Connell, Jessica St. Clair, Judi Watson, and Sue Winterbourne. Most especially we want to thank Peggy Pelonis for her many contributions to this book, and her care, collegiality, interest, and leadership in making Adlerian therapy a functional training experience in Athens, Greece. We also want to thank Gerald and Marianne Corey, our friends and colleagues, who have kept Adlerian group counseling in the forefront of counselor education, and who, over many years, have made it possible for us to offer our ideas and therapeutic processes to countless students and professionals. And finally, we want to acknowledge the people associated with Brunner-Routledge who made this book a reality, especially Emily Epstein Loeb and Erin Herlihy, our editors, and the extremely useful reviews provided by Drs. Thomas Sweeney at the University of North Carolina at Greensboro and Jon Carlson at Governors State University.

Manford A. Sonstegard: The Man and His Therapy

An Introduction by James Robert Bitter

I first met Dr. Manford A. Sonstegard in 1974. He was 63 years old, and he had already served as a teacher, counselor, principal, consultant, and counselor educator. Following the lead of his great teacher, Rudolf Dreikurs, he had helped to establish Family Education Centers in five different states, parts of the Caribbean, Europe, and Africa, where he had also served as an educational consultant to the government of Ethiopia. In addition, he had developed Dreikurs' (1960) teleoanalytic approach to group counseling into a comprehensive art form with a fully developed process and practice (Dreikurs & Sonstegard, 1967, 1968a, 1968b; Sonstegard & Dreikurs, 1973). Sonstegard would eventually update his group chapter with Dreikurs twice (Sonstegard & Dreikurs, 1975; Sonstegard, Dreikurs, & Bitter, 1982).

In 1974, I was completing doctoral studies at Idaho State University and coordinating the first Conference on Adlerian Psychology to be held at that university. Dr. Steven Feit recommended Sonstegard. Dr. Feit, a graduate of West Virginia University, had taken a course or two from "Sonste" before joining the faculty in the Department of Counselor Education at Idaho State University. Sonste was able to present in a number of different areas, but my main interest was in his work with groups. I asked him if he would be willing to do some group counseling demonstrations and discuss the process of Adlerian group counseling and psychotherapy. His affirmative answer included a request for "adolescents who were not 'A' students."

"Really good students always volunteer," he said, "but they do not make for the most interesting of demonstrations. Young people with

xv

some difficulties have something to gain, and therefore, they have much to offer."

"Fine," I said. "I will find you the worst kids we can round up." And that is exactly what I did. I went to all of the area schools, and teachers recommended students who were failing or in trouble at school or with the law; all of the original eight students had turned disruption into an art form. Not all of the original eight showed up, but the five who did had exactly two 1 $^{1}/_{2}$-hour group sessions, one on stage in front of almost 400 people who were attending the conference. In *Adlerian Group Counseling & Therapy: Step by Step* (chap. 2), one of these sessions is completely delineated with our commentary.

The conference lasted 4 days, and the group sessions changed the lives of five adolescents. They followed Dr. Sonstegard around for the full time he was there, eating meals with him and buying him presents. He listened, and he helped them with whatever they brought for his consideration. Six-month and 1-year follow-ups with teachers and parents indicated the changes with these five students were holding.

I completed my doctoral studies in 1974, and in September of that year I was lucky enough to secure a faculty position in the Counseling Program chaired by Dr. Sonstegard at what is now the Marshall University Graduate College in Charleston, West Virginia. He came to my office the first morning that I was on the job. I was unpacking boxes of books. He said, "Come on. We're going to a school to do some counseling."

As we headed to a small mountain community about 30 miles from Charleston, my training as a counselor educator began. He would eventually cover everything from counseling process and collaborative consultation to in vivo supervision (Dreikurs & Sonstegard, 1966), but he started with a commentary on breakfast. "Look at that young man eating potato chips and drinking a Coke as he heads out to work in the fields. I would never hire him. He needs protein, or he won't have enough energy to get to the afternoon."

His comments were somewhat disconcerting to me, because that is exactly what I had ingested an hour earlier. We arrived at the school, greeted the principal and a couple of teachers Sonste already knew, and went to work. In a small room off the cafeteria, there were five adolescents and two graduate students waiting to meet with us. Sonste introduced one of the graduate students to the group of teenagers and asked them if this student might talk with them for a while. Then he indicated to the student that she might start.

Although she mostly gathered information from these young people initially, I remember thinking that she was more confident than I would have been in her shoes. About 20 minutes into the session, she stopped to ask Sonste what she should do next. He simply asked her: "What do you make out of Tom's concern that people are always picking on him and he gets so angry?" The graduate student felt that maybe Tom felt hurt. In turn, Sonste asked the other graduate student and then each of the group members. When he got to me, I thought I had heard some pretty good hunches and could think of nothing new to offer.

"I have another idea," Sonste noted. "Would you like to hear it? I think Tom gets picked on, because everyone knows that he is an easy target. He expects to be mistreated, and he goes off at the slightest provocation—like a firecracker on the fourth of July."

It was the first time I had ever seen a group *recognition reflex*. His own peers instantly confirmed how they often "pushed" Tom and "taunted" him just to get a rise out of him. Even Tom acknowledged that he went off easily. Still, Sonste did not let this become a group discussion of Tom, the victim. He engaged all of us in a discussion of the goals and purposes of peer abuse. Even back then, he was attempting to reclaim those who felt marginalized and excluded by those in favored group positions, an effort he continues to pursue in his work today (Sonstegard, Bitter, & Pelonis-Peneros, 2001).

On the way home, he asked me what I thought about the morning. I told him that I had learned a lot, but I didn't feel I had much to offer.

"Nonsense," he said. "You were there, and you made a contribution. The graduate student who started the group spent the last two semesters watching me lead groups. This was her first time to begin a group on her own. She will co-lead with us for this semester, and then next semester, she may be ready to start her own group with weekly supervision and only periodic interventions by us." Then with a wry smile: "It takes time to prepare and train good group leaders."

"Let me guess," I said. "It all starts with a good breakfast."

Thus, I began a friendship and working relationship that has lasted more than a quarter of a century. In the early years, I had as much to learn as any of his graduate students. I had read a great deal, but I lacked experience and adequate supervision. Sonste trained me without ever letting me feel less than a colleague in good standing. He took me with him everywhere he went: to schools and community agencies, on consultation trips to many different cities, and to conventions where we would present new material and offer demonstrations. Initially, I watched and asked a lot of questions. In a very short period of time, however, he was having me do the work, intervening when necessary, but giving me lots of freedom to experiment and develop my own style.

Sonste was then, and is now, the single greatest teacher I ever had. He was not just *good* at his work. He was a model for everything he taught. Like many people, I have had *to learn* the principles of Adlerian psychology and develop a community feeling with social interest. In Sonste, these attributes have always been a natural part of his very being. When he met Dreikurs, what he learned really affirmed what he already believed—what he already "lived."

Adlerians believe that all behavior occurs in a social context and is, therefore, interpersonally motivated and best understood systemically. In this sense, Adlerian counselors and therapists attempt to understand individuals holistically. We are not interested in studying human beings as a set of parts, but rather seek to know the whole person as she or he moves through life. Young children, experiencing a normal feeling of inferiority, strive for a better position—for competence and mastery. These early strivings can be understood as movements toward immediate goals: movements that may be *conscious* or *unconscious* (Adlerians use these terms as adjectives rather than as nouns representing reified states of mind). Eventually, individuals develop more long-term goals of completion, actualization, or perfection, and these life goals unify our personality such that every thought, feeling, action, belief, conviction, and value can be understood to be part of the *movement* toward our fictional endpoints.

This individual movement toward a life goal is what Adlerians call one's style of living or *lifestyle*. Because we are social beings, our movement through life is heavily influenced by heredity and environment. Both heredity and environment, however, are less important than the interpretations that people make of these influences. The family, for example, is an enormous influence on who we are, but neither the model set by our parents nor the birth position we hold in the family is as important as the meaning that each person assigns to these experiences. We all interpret life and then seek a place in it. How we claim that place in life defines much of our value and worth to others. We have the freedom to choose.

Because we can choose who we will be and how we will act, Adler (1931/1958) noted that it was possible for people to develop on either the useless side of life or the useful side. The former almost always includes mistaken notions about self, others, and the world. This useless side involves pessimism, self-absorption, and goals of superiority in relation to others. The useful side, on the other hand, is characterized by what Adler called a *community feeling*, a sense of belonging to the community of human beings past, present, and future. Such a feeling is innate and must be developed in the young: It is enacted through what Adlerians call *social interest*, an interest in the welfare of others that is just as important as our own well-being. People with this kind of social interest feel connected to others. They meet the universal tasks of life with courage, confidence (optimism), and a sense of humor. They find life meaningful, and they assign significance to others as well as self. This allows them to facilitate the growth of others, because they have learned to get along with themselves (Mosak, 2000).

Over the years, Sonste's total congruence with the Adlerian model has helped him train counselors and therapists in the United States and Canada as well as in Africa, Europe, and South America. He has trained and supervised professionals and paraprofessionals in individual, couples, and family counseling, working with all ages and with multiple cultures. His most consistent interests, however, have remained with the practice and supervision of Adlerian group counseling and therapy.

In 1996, an interview in the *Journal for Specialists in Group Work* highlighted the life and work of Sonstegard (Bitter, 1996). This book grew out of that initial effort and is an attempt to offer our readers a measure of the genius and therapeutic gifts people witness in Sonste's work. Similar to his style of training, the book is divided into two parts. The first part is intended to engage the reader experientially, almost as if you might be watching Sonste lead a group. It starts with a brief rationale for group process (chap. 1) followed immediately by an actual typescript of a group experience with adolescents that Sonste conducted in Idaho (chap. 2). That typescript is arranged so that you can see our commentary on the group experience as you read. We recommend that you read the whole group transcript first without commentary and then review it again with commentary on our thinking and purposeful interventions. The second part of the book presents the theoretical foundations that underlie our approach and model. In chapter 3, we present the basic theory, structure, and flow of Adlerian group counseling and therapy. Because we believe that adolescents function psychologically in ways similar to adults—albeit with less experience in the world and their own developmental issues—we provide the essential practice guidelines for Adlerian group counseling and therapy in chapter 4. This is followed by the special considerations we bring to group counseling with children (chap. 5). Part II concludes with our thoughts about the training, education, and supervision of group counselors and group therapists (chap. 6).

At the age of 92, Sonstegard is working with counselors in England, training parents and teachers, and running groups for adolescents. He lives with his wife Rita in the English countryside where they have been since moving there in 1997. "It's an adventure," he told me just before he left the United States. "Sometimes, we have to let go of everything we have, of everything we know and all that is safe and familiar; life happens now and in the future, and we have to go out to meet it."

REFERENCES

Adler, A. (1958). *What life should mean to you.* New York: Capricorn. (Original work published 1931)

Bitter, J. (1996). Manford A. Sonstegard: A career in group counseling. *Journal for Specialists in Group Work, 21*(3), 194–213.

Dreikurs, R. (1960). *Group psychotherapy and group approaches: Collected papers of Rudolf Dreikurs.* Chicago: Alfred Adler Institute.

Dreikurs, R., & Sonstegard, M. A. (1966). A specific approach to practicum supervision. *Counselor Education and Supervision, 6,* 18–25.

Dreikurs, R., & Sonstegard, M. A. (1967). *The teleoanalytic approach to group counseling.* Chicago: Alfred Adler Institute.

Dreikurs, R., & Sonstegard, M. A. (1968a). The Adlerian or teleoanalytic group counseling approach. In G. Gazda (Ed.), *Basic approaches to group psychotherapy and group counseling* (pp. 197–232). Springfield, IL: Charles C Thomas.

Dreikurs, R., & Sonstegard, M. A. (1968b). Rationale of group counseling. In D. Dinkmeyer (Ed.), *Guidance and counseling in the elementary school: Readings in theory and practice* (pp. 278–287). New York: Holt, Rinehart & Winston.

Mosak, H. H. (2000). Adlerian psychotherapy. In R. J. Corsini & D. Wedding (Eds.), *Current psychotherapies* (6th ed.) (pp. 54–98). Itasca, IL: F. E. Peacock.

Sonstegard, M. A., Bitter, J. R., & Pelonis-Peneros, P. P. (2001). From Cain to Columbine: A psychosocial analysis of violence. In Adlerian Society of the United Kingdom and the Institute for Individual Psychology (Eds.), *Yearbook 2001* (pp. 104–121). London: Editor.

Sonstegard, M. A., & Dreikurs, R. (1973). The Adlerian approach to group counseling of children. In M. M. Ohlsen (Ed.), *Counseling children in groups: A forum* (pp. 47–77). New York: Holt, Rinehart & Winston.

Sonstegard, M. A., & Dreikurs, R. (1975). The teleoanalytic group counseling approach. In G. Gazda (Ed.), *Basic approaches to group psychotherapy and group counseling* (2nd ed., pp. 468–510). Springfield, IL: Charles C Thomas.

Sonstegard, M. A., Dreikurs, R., & Bitter, J. R. (1982). The teleoanalytic group counseling approach. In G. Gazda (Ed.), *Basic approaches to group psychotherapy and group counseling* (3rd ed., pp. 507–551). Springfield, IL: Charles C Thomas.

Part I

The Process and Practice of Adlerian Group Counseling and Therapy

CHAPTER 1

A Rationale for Adlerian Group Work[1]

In this chapter, we:

- Discuss the importance of the group in the formation of human life;
- Delineate the interrelationship of democracy and group work;
- Consider group counseling and therapy as:
  - Experiential learning.
  - A foundation for the development of voice.
  - A venue for social support.
  - A context for both personal and interactive meaning.
  - A process for values clarification and formation.
  - A structure for the implementation of democratic process.

Every child is born into a group. In most cases, this group is the family, but even in alternative situations, a child needs a group to survive. The child's early helplessness parallels the individual inferiorities of early humans. Adler (1957) was the first to suggest that Darwin's (1976) imperatives for survival of the species had a concomitant psychological stance in the human condition. In comparison to other animals, early humans had poor eyesight, dull claws, insensitive hearing, and slowness of movement. Like other species with individual weaknesses, human survived by forming into a herd, dividing the labor, and eventually building a community. The psychological stances that supported this group formation were a feeling of belonging and interdependence; nurturance, friendship, and support; mutual respect; and cooperation and loyalty: the same things that a child requires to live and grow. Just as the family must adjust to accommodate each new child, each child must develop her or his own unique place and approach to integration within the group. The methods chosen by each person are in keeping with the individual's self-concept and interpretation of life. The family is the first group in which most people must find a place. As the child extends her- or himself into new realms (the school, and ultimately the community), the struggle to belong broadens, with one's peer group often becoming the strongest force.

One of the great paradoxes within the human condition is that cooperation within a group does not necessarily imply cooperation between groups. That is, cooperation and competition can exist simultaneously. This can be seen in a positive sense when two sporting teams take the field, each team cooperating as a unit or group while competing with the other. It can also exist in a negative sense: two inner city gangs at war, for example, or when a group experiencing discrimination bonds together, but simultaneously discriminates against another, perhaps less fortunate, group. What Dreikurs (1971) used to call the "war between the sexes" and the "war between the generations" reflect this tendency of humans in like condition to come together and to cooperate within the group while competing with those on the outside. Indeed, it is often a group-defined "outside force or threat" that motivates the formation and maintenance processes of a group.

In previous centuries, two conditions contributed to a greater ease in children discovering and adapting to their place. Both of these conditions began to erode with the development of an industrialized, and increasingly technological, urban society. The effects, however, were still evident even as late as the middle of the 20th century.[2]

A Rationale for Adlerian Group Work

The first condition extended from our long history of human autocratic and totalitarian states; whether these governments were aristocracies or male-dominated ideological systems, the regulatory procedures placed a high priority on *control*. Rigid hierarchies, defined by axioms of superiority and inferiority or ideological necessity, used authoritarian processes to institutionalize and maintain that control. Children born into these systems had very little choice about how they would develop, to which stratum they would belong, and with which group they would identify. If any person, child or adult, attempted to "get beyond themselves," all the mechanisms of the strata above—and even the government itself—could be exercised to keep a person in his or her place.

The second condition pertained to those societies that were essentially agrarian. In these societies, large families were both necessary and the norm. The outside forces against which families organized were the weather, seasonal requirements, pests, and disease and injuries affecting people, animals, or crops. Here again, children were taught essential tasks early. They knew how they fit into the system, and they had a place well before they reached what we now call "adolescence."[3]

Political freedom and social democracy always augment options and increase the fluidity of individual movement between socioeconomic strata. Education and technology are the means by which both individual and group options are most often actualized. An increase in personal freedom and social equality, however, does not imply that people are prepared to handle these benefits or their effects; this is especially true for children. Where order and place are no longer predetermined, each individual must struggle with multiple possibilities to create a place for oneself.

Still, each child starts in a given group, and each child both influences and is influenced by the members of that group—before moving on to other groups in which the child will again exchange influences. People may change the groups with which they associate many times over a lifetime. In each case, they will leave their mark, and they will also change. The impact of the group on each child is easily observed whenever the child participates in that group. The use of the group to influence the child constitutes not only an effective means of teaching, but also an effective way to offer corrective influences (Dreikurs, 1957; Sonstegard, 1968).

At the end of the 20th century, democracies are exploding across the political landscape. Group techniques are more imperative now than ever before; in each of these political democracies, the authority of the privileged individual is being replaced with the authority of the group. The group is ultimately the reality in which all of us will operate.

Every time democracies begin to emerge, group methods in one form or another come into vogue. Socrates used a form of group counseling with youth that consisted basically of reorientation by means of well-framed questions. Aristotle, too, was aware of the cathartic effect of theater, both for the group of participants and for the audience (Copleston, 1959).

In the twentieth century, group counseling and therapy has codeveloped with the psychological professions. It had its beginning in Europe at the turn of the century, and it reached its peak in the two and a half decades following World War II. During this same period, every time a country retreated from democracy (into totalitarianism), group procedures were totally abandoned: This happened in much of Europe during the World Wars and in all of the Eastern Europe with the formation of the Communist block. It is not surprising, therefore, that group process and practice has developed most rapidly in the United States. For not only does group process require a democratic atmosphere, it creates one.

Adler appears to have been the first psychiatrist to use group methods deliberately and systematically in his child guidance clinics in Vienna[4] (Hoffman, 1994). They were not clinics as we think of them in an era of managed care. Adler met with groups of teachers and the parents of the children these teachers served. His most common procedure involved a careful consideration of data provided by educators before interviewing children and parents in the presence of other community members. Because Adler initiated his open-forum process in school settings, his group counseling approach has always been applicable to education.

There was, quite naturally, opposition to and criticism of group approaches that was proffered by those who favored individual therapy. Group therapy flew in the face of the strong Freudian contention that mental illness and maladjustment resulted from intrapsychic conflicts within the individual (Freud, 1964). If this contention were true, there would clearly be no need for group counseling; it should have no effect: It might even be harmful.

Adler (1935/1996a, 1935/1996b) advanced a social psychology in which neuroses and other psychological disturbances were understood to be retreats from the requirements of social living, avoidances of personal failure, and reflections of uncertainty about one's place among fellow humans. In contrast, Adler saw human well-being as grounded in a community feeling and implemented with social interest and self-determination. Dreikurs (1971) enlarged Adler's "ironclad logic of social living" with an emphasis on social equality as the basis for cooperation and social harmony. Both Adler and Dreikurs believed in the unity of the personality and a socio-teleological determination of human behavior. These Adlerian postulates define the intrinsic power and strength of the individual as centered within the group.

Children, adolescents, and even adults may appear deficient or weak when they become discouraged or lose self-confidence. From a teleological perspective, these people are merely using useless methods to find a place. Whether a person is described as "good" or "bad," "right" or "wrong," "strong" or "weak," that person is better understood as attempting to reach some self-selected goal or set of goals.

Recognizing that the problems of individuals are essentially social gives group counseling its special significance—in terms of both diagnosis and remediation. In the action and interaction within each group, individuals express their goals, their sense of belonging, their intentions and social connectedness.

Adler's systemic orientation has gained credence in the last 25 years. In his lifetime, however, he was in constant conflict with mechanistic approaches to behavior that sought to establish causal relationships based on heredity and biological endowment or environmental stimulus. These modern positions found their parallel in the search for human essences, the factors that made humans functional or dysfunctional, good or bad, superior or inferior. With the emergence of democratic evolution, environmental influence gained a foothold in the "essence" battle for a short while, but neither heredity nor environment ever fully explained human process and human development. There has been a reemphasis on hermeneutics in the last half of the twentieth century, a validation of the value of Adler's psychological teleology: Humans are understood to formulate individual goals and to use the "givens" in their heredity or environment in accordance with these purposes and the private logic that supports them.

The recent emergence of postmodern viewpoints has reasserted an awareness of superiority and inferiority, of dominance and submission (Foucault, 1994; Gergen, 1991; McNamee & Gergen, 1992). White and Epston's (1990) narrative therapy is designed to help individuals take a stand against problematic hermeneutics and imperatives from a dominant culture. None of the postmodern approaches could be realized outside of a democratic society, without the possibility of freedom and social equality. Indeed, social constructionism is based on the recognition that the power to "make" a person or system perform, behave, or conform has already diminished; it has become increasingly difficult and often impossible.

As each person achieves a socially equal status, inner motivation becomes more important than pressure from without. Even inner motivation is socially constructed. When the authority of dominant culture positions (e.g., men over women, White European over people of color, adults over children) diminishes, the group that constitutes one's peers gains in importance. In a democracy, the relationship of individual to dominant culture is always interactive. Although it is easy to observe the impact of dominant culture on the individual, the influence of the individual on those who represent dominant culture is often missed. It is not uncommon, however, for those representing a dominant position (e.g., teachers, parents, or White male "leaders") to react in line with the intentions of those they seek to subvert (Dreikurs, 1971). An effective counseling approach must serve to clarify the nature of interaction, and, if necessary, to improve it.

Group therapy and group counseling are natural tools for addressing relationships. In the group, members can experiment with interactions and produce changes in the mistaken goals and notions that an individual is pursuing. The history of counseling and psychotherapy has been predicated on the assumption that privacy is an indispensable requirement. But the need for privacy fits better with an authoritarian era when a troubled individual approached an expert in shame, hoping for relief. Privacy forced people to live "lives of quiet desperation" (Thoreau, 1968, p. 8) and to reside in an atmosphere of emotional isolation—ever fearful that one's deficiencies would be discovered. Indeed, it was always the fear inside that clamored for privacy, reflecting a lack of mutual trust or of a feeling of belonging and a retreat to a safe distance. Group counseling and group psychotherapy shatter privacy; they stand in opposition to isolation and transform individual problems into common concerns. Group counseling, however, is more than mere assistance for individuals. It becomes a social force in a culture in transition from dominant to egalitarian. It promotes new social realities and fortifies newly emerging cultural possibilities. Group counseling is both a product of a democratic evolution and a tool for meeting its needs.

Group counseling is experiential learning. For learning to stick, for an education to have meaning in one's life, it must result in use, in action, in experience. In a group, participation is the action that is necessary for learning to occur. Without participation in the group by the members, no therapy can result. Participation is not always verbal or assertive. There are many cases in which youngsters would have withdrawn, and perhaps left the group, if they were pushed to interact verbally. Group process allows members to interact uniquely and individually, sometimes only with a smile, a twinkle in the eye, a nod, or a silent gesture. In individual therapy, learning almost always requires some verbal interaction with the therapist. In group counseling, a withdrawn or quiet member can often learn much by merely listening to others.

Still, group counseling encourages the development of voice. Carol Gilligan's (1982) important studies helped us to realize that girls and boys develop in different realities, function with different moral codes (Gilligan, 1982; Gilligan, Ward, Taylor, & Bardige, 1988), and seek different ends in relationship. Group counseling bridges the gap in developmental processes, offers equal opportunities for participation, and validates unique contributions. As group members identify with each other and come to understand diverse feelings and motivations, acceptance leads to more active participation. Universalization results and becomes the cementing element in group cohesiveness. Interactions in effective group sessions often help each member to "find a voice," to take a stand, and to integrate certain ideas that were previously unacceptable to some individual's thinking.

Group counseling is support. In groups, the leader is almost always less important than the members. It is the members who begin to help each other, for participation in a group almost automatically evokes mutual support. Most of the social situations in which we live remain competitive in nature, and the individual is engaged in winning or self-elevation. This is true in too many homes, most schools, some forms of recreation and sport, and almost all fundamental religious activities. Under these conditions, there is little possibility of assuming responsibility for one another, of counteracting social isolation, or of making a commitment to the well-being of one's peers.

Two girls in the same classroom had an interest in riding horses. One had a horse and rode frequently. The other had no horse and had never ridden. In most classrooms—indeed, in most communities—these two would never meet in a manner that facilitated a relationship. In group, Alice listens to Karen express her unfulfilled desire to ride. "You can come riding with me sometime," Alice says. "Why haven't you asked me before?"

"Oh, I couldn't do that," Karen answers.

"Why not?"
"I didn't even know you."
"But we were in the same class."
"Yes, but I didn't really know you."
"Well, now you do."

When a group member says, "I will help you if you like," we immediately know two things: (a) The group member who has offered the help has found a place in the group and is likely on the way to finding a place in the larger world, and (b) the help will be offered to a peer because of social interest and not merely to elevate oneself personally.

The group invests social situations with real meaning. Some people never have an opportunity to test themselves in real social situations. They find ways to hold themselves back, letting life happen without much involvement at all. They may talk about life without ever fully experiencing it (Polster & Polster, 1973). Groups, however, are close and often temporarily limited social units. The problems that each person reveals cannot be ignored. They are owned by the group and must be solved by the group. The contribution that each person makes is essential, even if it comes in the form of silent and mostly nonverbal support.

When social equality is established in group therapy, deficiencies lose their stigma. Even when difficulties are a necessary qualification for membership in a group (e.g., group counseling for underachievers or for those who are depressed), there need not be any loss of social status. Every one starts out in the same position, and everyone counts.

Group counseling is values-forming. While individual therapy can proceed for months without initiating changes in one's values, group counseling cannot avoid dealing with values. All human values, beliefs, convictions, and codes are social in nature, and social participation both reveals the stance of members and challenges their usefulness. Most of the rest of life (families, schools, work, and community) seeks to instill the dominant knowledge-positions and the values of the system; these same influences work to minimize alternative points of view and nontraditional voices.

When a dominant culture cannot address or handle faulty behavior, its representatives usually increase the very interventions that have already failed to bring about change. They actually fortify the useless behaviors and the values that support them. Group counseling puts a faulty value system on trial and allows correction to be implemented without blame.

Bradley is in the third grade. His parents have taken him to the doctor for several consultations, because they believe he is unable to eat solid food. He will also not get out of bed in the morning and requires his parents to get him dressed if he is to get to school. None of these facts, however, are known to the counselor or the group members.

Bradley: This morning I woke up when I heard the mixer.
Ali: The mixer?
Bradley: Yes, my mother was making a milkshake for me.
Dallas: A milkshake for breakfast? Cool!
Bradley: My mother always fixes a milkshake for me. Then she brings it to me in bed.
Ali: You eat in bed?
Bradley: While I am drinking my milkshake, my mother also gets a bath ready for me, and then she dresses me. I think of her kind of like a servant.
Counselor: How many of you have breakfast brought to you in bed?
Thomas: I haven't ever eaten in bed, not even when I was a baby. I always get up for breakfast.
Ali: I always get up too.
Annie: I've never heard of a milkshake for breakfast, and I usually take my own bath before I go to bed. I've done that ever since I was big.

The counseling session turned to other topics. We know from other sources that Bradley soon started getting up in the morning and eating breakfast with his father. We also know from his teachers that his participation in classroom activities increased, most notably in arithmetic.

Group counseling is structural. In individual therapy, structure is easily discernible and is largely the responsibility of the therapist (Corey, 2001). In group counseling, structure is neither obvious nor can it be implemented solely by the counselor. Structure brings order to human interactions. Without it, the group process becomes confused and chaotic. Group counseling requires that the members engage with the group leader in the act of cocreating structure. The cocreation process serves democracy well; it acts as a corrective agent to all of the systems of control in which members have been raised.

Group counseling is facilitated best by experienced leadership. The fact that an experienced leader anticipates a usual process or structure to a group is not the same as controlling the group. This anticipation merely gives the leader a place to start and does not surprise her or him as the process develops. There are many different configurations that have been used to describe group process (see Corey & Corey, 2002, or Yalom, 1995). Adlerians work in many different modes, but they anticipate that groups will (a) form and maintain an interactive relationship, the more therapeutic of which are characterized by acceptance and mutual respect; (b) examine purposes and motivations underlying member actions and behaviors—replacing criticism with understanding; (c) help individuals to understand the goals they may be pursuing through tentative psychological disclosures; and (d) support reorientation and redirection when a member's life warrants it (Sonstegard, Dreikurs, & Bitter, 1982). Although the leadership for group process should clearly remain with the most experienced person in the beginning, group members commonly assert varying levels of leadership as the group progresses. The interventions of the designated leader often become less as members begin to handle the process themselves.

Developing an effective counseling relationship is more than merely establishing "good" relationships. The group counselor must model the process of listening and understanding that facilitates a democratic atmosphere. Although Adlerians believe that this relationship is based on mutual respect, this stance does not imply that members may do anything they please. Firmness and kindness are essential qualities. When disruptive interactions occur, it is the counselor who must direct the discussion toward a discovery of purpose and the life goals that are sought. It is the counselor who reminds the group members that they do not have to merely react, but can create possibilities that might lead to real change. A group counselor knows that people need encouragement and function best when encouraged; the leader looks for opportunities to invoke encouragement from group members, because the statements and opinions of the group tend to carry more weight that anything the counselor can say.

The psychological professions that use counseling and psychotherapy are entering into an era when there is more to do and fewer resources with which to do them. Community agencies and community mental health centers are increasingly organized as managed care systems. Once individuals have been seen for an initial evaluation, crisis intervention is the most likely response; those who need ongoing therapy may experience significant delays in making contact with a counselor or therapist. Similarly, school consolidation, shrinking resources, and augmented birth rates have greatly increased the number of students in a school counselor's care: The ratio can easily be greater than 500 to 1. Some school districts have been forced to terminate counseling programs altogether, especially at the elementary level. Most states have some districts in which a single counselor travels to three or four schools every week. Even psychotherapeutic approaches designed to address the concerns of single units (e.g., family or marital therapy) must accommodate to a greater demand from the general public.

In each of these areas, group counseling and therapy is an answer whose time has come. Even if clients need initial evaluations and crisis intervention, groups provide agencies and schools with a means of offering services to a larger number of individuals on an ongoing basis. Where group counseling and psychotherapy were once used as adjuncts to individual therapy, the reality of delivering mental health services to growing populations will quickly make group therapy a treatment of choice. Even those who primarily serve couples and families have found groups useful in ensuring treatment efficacy (Carlson, Sperry, & Lewis, 1997; Christensen, 1993).

Adlerian group counseling is perhaps better positioned than most approaches to meet the needs of people in the new millennium. Adlerians have been using group methods for most of the 20th century. Teleological interventions have been devised for a wide population, including very young children, school-age children, adolescents, college students, and adults. Adlerian group methods have been used in community agencies, hospitals, clinics, and schools (Dinkmeyer, Dinkmeyer, & Sperry, 1987). The Adlerian approach is the basis for at least one school consultation model (Dinkmeyer & Carlson, 2001); it is also the foundation for the largest parent education [i.e., *STEP* (Dinkmeyer & McKay, 1997) and *Active Parenting* (Popkin, 1993)] and teacher education (Albert, 1996) programs in the United States. It is still the only approach to have created open-forum family education centers (Christensen, 1993) to serve groups of parents and their children. Whether the need is remedial or preventative, Adlerian group counseling processes have been developed, and practitioners are available to demonstrate the effectiveness of the model.

SUMMARY

In this chapter, we have provided a specific rationale for Adlerian group work and for the use of group processes in democratic societies.

Group counseling and therapy build on the natural group experiences of the family, one's peers, and the community by providing a safe, accepting, and encouraging place in which ones ideas, feelings, and behaviors can be reconsidered within a social context where individual concerns are addressed as community issues. In this sense, groups are experiential learning systems that encourage the individual development of voice as well as a community feeling characterized by contribution, connection, and commitment to others. Groups provide social support and invest real interactions and problem solving with meaning. Groups are a venue in which values are clarified and formed, and they provide a structure for experiencing the very foundation of democratic process.

REFERENCES

Adler, A. (1957). *Understanding human nature* (W. B. Wolfe, Trans.). New York: Premier Books. (Original work published 1927)

Adler, A. (1996a). The structure of neurosis. *Individual Psychology, 52*(4), 351–362. (Original work published 1935)

Adler, A. (1996b). What is neurosis? *Individual Psychology, 52*(4), 318–333. (Original work published 1935)

Albert, L. (1996). *Cooperative discipline.* Circle Pines, MN: American Guidance Service.

Carlson, J., Sperry, L., & Lewis, J. A. (1997). *Family therapy: Ensuring treatment efficacy.* Pacific Grove, CA: Brooks/Cole.

Christensen, O. C. (Ed.). (1993). *Adlerian family counseling* (rev. ed.). Minneapolis, MN: Educational Media Corp.

Copleston, F. (1959). *A history of philosophy: Volume I: Greece and Rome* (rev. ed.). Westminister, MD: Newman Press.

Corey, G. (2001). *Theory and practice of counseling and psychotherapy* (6th ed.). Pacific Grove, CA: Brooks/Cole.

Corey, M. S., & Corey, G. (2002). *Groups: Process and practice* (6th ed.). Pacific Grove, CA: Brooks/Cole.

Darwin, C. G. (1976). *On the origin of the species: By means of natural selection or the preservation of favored races in the struggle for life.* Norwalk, CT: Easton Press. (Original work published 1859)

Dinkmeyer, D. C., Jr., & Carlson, J. (2001). *Consultation: Creating school-based interventions.* Philadelphia: Brunner-Routledge.

Dinkmeyer, Sr., D. C., Dinkmeyer, D. C., Jr., & Sperry, L. (1987). *Adlerian counseling and psychotherapy* (2nd ed.). Columbus, OH: Merrill.

Dinkmeyer, D. C., & McKay, G. D. (1997). *Systematic training for effective parenting* [STEP] (rev. ed.). Circle Pines, MN: American Guidance Service.

Dreikurs, R. (1957). Psychotherapy as correction of faulty social values. *Journal of Individual Psychology, 13,* 150–158.

Dreikurs, R. (1971). *Social equality: The challenge of today.* Chicago: Henry Regnery. (Original work published 1961)

Foucault, M. (1994). *The order of things: An archaeology of the human sciences.* New York: Vintage Books. (Original work published 1966)

Freud, S. (1964). *Complete works.* London: Hogarth Press.

Gergen, K. (1991). *The saturated self.* New York: Basic Books.

Gilligan, C. (1982). *In a different voice: Psychological theory and women's development.* Cambridge, MA: Harvard University Press.

Gilligan, C., Ward, J. V., Taylor, J. M., with Bardige, B. (1988). *Mapping the moral domain.* Cambridge, MA: Harvard University Press.

Hoffman, E. (1994). *The drive for self: Alfred Adler and the founding of individual psychology.* Reading, MA: Addison Wesley.

McNamee, S., & Gergen, K. J. (Eds.). (1992). *Therapy as social construction.* Newbury Park, CA: Sage.

Polster, E., & Polster, M. (1973). *Gestalt therapy integrated: Contours of theory and practice.* New York: Random House.

Popkin, M. H. (1993). *Active parenting today.* Atlanta, GA: Active Parenting.

Sonstegard, M. A. (1968). Mechanisms and practical techniques in group counseling in the elementary school. In J. J. Muro & S. L. Freeman (Eds.), *Readings in group counseling* (pp. 127–136). Scranton, PA: International Textbook.

Sonstegard, M. A. (1998). A rationale for group counseling. *Journal of Individual Psychology, 54*(2), 164–175.

Sonstegard, M. A., Dreikurs, R., & Bitter, J. R. (1982). The teleoanalytic group counseling approach. In G. Gazda (Ed.), *Basic approaches to group psychotherapy and group counseling* (3rd ed., pp. 507–551). Springfield, IL: Charles C Thomas.

Thoreau, H. D. (1968). *The writings of Henry David Thoreau: Volume 2: Walden.* New York: AMS Press.

White, M., & Epston, D. (1990). *Narrative means to therapeutic ends.* New York: Norton. (Original work published 1989)

Yalom, I. D. (1995). *The theory and practice of group psychotherapy* (4th ed.). New York: Basic Books.

NOTES

1. This chapter appeared in a slightly different form in Sonstegard, M. A. (1998), A rationale for group counseling. *Journal of Individual Psychology, 54*(2), 164–175. Reprinted with permission from University of Texas Press.
2. From the early 1900s to the late 1960s, 70% of the population in the United States moved from farms and small communities to the cities.

3. The concept of adolescence was really born with the advent of developmental psychology in the 1940s. Our ideas about children as growing human organisms are not yet two-thirds of a century old. The concept of development requires a life and world in which there is time to grow up, in which the majority of human effort is no longer aimed at mere survival. It is only in the last half of the 20th century that the United States achieves such a world for the majority of its people.
4. All of Adler's child guidance clinics were closed with the advent of the Third Reich.

CHAPTER 2

Adlerian Group Counseling and Therapy: Step by Step

In this chapter, we:

- Provide an edited typescript **(in bold lettering)** of an actual group counseling session conducted by Dr. Manford Sonstegard;
- A *commentary* (*in italics*) on the interactions and process of the group experience as well as an explanation of the more important choice points and interventions used by the group leader.

In 1974, five adolescents from a small town in Idaho were invited to participate as members of a group counseling demonstration at a Conference on Adlerian Psychology with the theme of "motivation modification." Dr. Manford Sonstegard was the counselor. He had no previous contact with the group members, and he met all of them for the first time at the videotaped session. After a brief introduction to Adlerian process and practice, Dr. Sonstegard began the session.

The five group members are Hugh, Beth, John, Erv, and Karen. Erv and John are seated to Dr. Sonstegard's left, and Karen, Hugh, and Beth (in that order) are on his right. The group is roughly in a horseshoe shape with the counselor at the open end. The placement of the cameras leaves a considerable gap between Beth and John. The five people in this group go to the same high school, and they all know each other to some degree.

Even though this group session is intended to be a videotaped demonstration, Dr. Sonstegard starts the session as he would with any ongoing group that he is meeting for the first time. Because he does not believe there is any value to prescreening meetings, he has welcomed anyone who is willing to participate.

As we noted in the first chapter, groups are essentially exercises in democracy; indeed, it is unlikely that group counseling or therapy would be very effective outside of a democracy. A group democracy does not mean that all members are the same or have the same capabilities; hopefully, the group leader knows more about group process than the other members. Democracy does mean that everyone in the group has an equal right to be valued and respected: In a very pragmatic sense, this group leader brings a nonjudgmental, accepting, and even appreciating attitude to the process and works to help every person gain a vital voice within the group. Group counseling presupposes that the members of the group will be both the recipients of therapy and the agents of change within the group (Dreikurs & Sonstegard, 1968; Sonstegard, Dreikurs, & Bitter, 1982).

The following group session is divided into a typescript of the session[1] **in bold print** and commentary *in italics*. The reader may find it useful to read the complete session first and then to read the session a second time with the accompanying commentary. Another Adlerian therapist might begin the group differently, focus the group around a different issue, respond to the group members at different times and in different ways, but most Adlerian group sessions follow the stages of counseling first outlined by Dreikurs (1967): forming a relationship, psychological investigation, psychological disclosure, and reorientation. In the next chapter, we delineate this basic structure further. The commentary here is designed to "break down" this particular session step by step. The first step in most Adlerian group sessions is to arrive at an understanding of how the group will proceed and the manner of conducting the sessions. This is especially important if the group will be meeting over an extended period of time.

FORMING A GROUP RELATIONSHIP

Sonstegard:
1. **We should probably come to some agreements before we get started. What agreements do we need?**

    *[Commentary] While the **prescreening** of group members is common today [and part of the professional guidelines for group counselors; ACA, 1995; ASGW, 1989], Adlerians typically reject the idea and the procedure. The process seems more designed for the protection of the therapist than the facilitation of the group. Too often, prescreening eliminates from the group the very person or people who could most use a group experience: the disruptive, the self-absorbed, and the isolated. We meet these people in society all the time; it does not safeguard the stronger members of the group to avoid difficult people or situations. Indeed, one or more of the stronger members may be able to make the difference that brings a problematic striving to the useful side of living.*

    *Adlerians start their groups by welcoming everyone and anyone and by seeking **agreements**. We do not use the words or concepts of rules or ground rules, both of which reflect and maintain our authoritarian history and the superior/inferior relationships inherent in that history. Democracies—and therefore groups—are based on the consent and agreement of those who choose to participate; we function and live by mutually established agreements with each other.*

Karen:
2. **How often should we meet?**

    [Commentary] Before Karen speaks, group members looked at each other; a short pause ensued. Karen was the first to respond after a beseeching glance, as if entreating them to speak. None did. It is not uncommon for the most nervous person to speak first, or for the person who wants things to go right or wants to act

responsibly. In either case, the leader must honor the contribution with recognition and response.

In this case, the leader makes a mental note that Karen appears to have a highly developed sense of responsibility. She would prefer others to take action, but because they don't, she feels it is up to her. At this stage, this interpretation is only a hypothesis to be verified or disproved as the session proceeds. Still, it is never too early for the leader to start gathering psychological hypotheses.

Sonstegard:
3. How often do you think we should meet? How often would you like to meet?

   [Commentary] The counselor turns all questions back to the group for a decision; this is not merely required for democratic purposes, but is essential for the establishment of group process. All group members—especially those who are adolescent—watch to see if the process is going to be group centered or leader centered. If the leader offers an opinion here, she or he risks losing the group members forever.

Hugh:
4. Wouldn't that depend on the problems we bring up? We might need to meet three times a week.

Sonstegard (clarifying):
5. Three times a week?

   [Commentary] Karen started with a very pragmatic question. The leader responds in a manner that keeps the answers pragmatic.

Hugh:
6. Maybe.

Sonstegard:
7. Well, what do all of you think of three times a week?

John:
8. I think three times a week is a little too much. Maybe once or twice a week, but three times is too much.

Beth:
9. I think that if someone has a problem they want to talk about, they should get in contact with the others, and we could talk then.

[Commentary] Beth's response may seem nonconsequential—or even thoughtful, but in terms of group process, it will inevitably distract from group decision making. She may also be signaling that she does not like to commit to a position until she knows the outcome.

Sonstegard (to Beth):
10. How often do you think we should meet as a group?
[Commentary] The leader redirects Beth back to the decision making at hand.

Beth:
11. As a group? Do you mean a regular planned meeting?

Sonstegard (nodding):
12. Yes.

Beth:
13. I think once a week would be enough.

Sonstegard:
14. Once a week?

Erv:
15. We could have emergency meetings.

Sonstegard:
16. Emergency meetings, right. We *could* call an emergency meeting if necessary.
(Pause)
Do you think we should start with once a week?
[Commentary] The leader, sensing a decision at hand, suggests what he believes to be the consensus of the group with a question. In an era when paraphrase, reflection, and summary are the staples of therapeutic interventions, the counselor often loses the empowerment inherent in honest and open questions. In this intervention, the leader's question requests an answer from the members as final authority.

Erv:
17. Yeah.

Sonstegard:
18. Are you willing to go along with once a week, Hugh?

Hugh:
19. Once a week would be fine ... depending on how long they last.
   [Commentary] Hugh indicates a new decision the group will need to make.

Sonstegard:
20. How long do you want them to last?
   [Commentary] The leader turns the decision back to the group, starting with the person who brings up the issue.

Hugh:
21. I think they would have to be ... well, it would depend on what you're talking about. If you are into something important, just go until you are through.

Beth:
22. Yeah, as long as it takes. If we don't have anything left to say, just quit.

Sonstegard (to Erv):
23. Do you have any opinion on this?
   [Commentary] Erv indicated a tentative willingness to participate in the last decision. The leader encourages him to participate in the second decision at a somewhat earlier stage.

Erv:
24. I don't think we can set a time limit: thirty minutes one day, maybe an hour and a half the next.

Sonstegard:
25. Can we leave it to the group each meeting to pick an appropriate time to stop?
   [Commentary] Again, the leader asks a question which seems to suggest the consensus of the group.

Erv:
26. Yeah.

Sonstegard:
27. Okay, then. What else should we agree on?

Hugh:
28. Well, we can't have a set topic each time. We may have different things on our minds.

Karen:
29. We should talk about whatever comes up.

Sonstegard:
30. You want it open-ended then.

Karen:
31. Yeah.

Sonstegard:
32. Do you all agree on that? (Heads nod) Well, that's okay with me.

John:
33. Is it okay if someone gets embarrassed or something ... (Pause) Is it okay if they leave for awhile?

[Commentary] John's question is both practical—in terms of group agreements—and personal: It may reflect earlier experiences in his life when he has needed some private space to collect himself. It could also indicate a personal priority (Kfir, 1981) or coping style that involves **control**, *because people with this priority often try to avoid humiliation or embarrassment: John's question starts another hypothesis forming in the counselor's mind.*

Sonstegard (to everyone):
34. Well, what do you think about that? Should people be permitted to leave and come back any time they want to do so?

Beth:
35. Yes, they should.

Sonstegard:
36. Think so?

Hugh:
37. We might be able to help if they stayed. If they stayed longer, we could talk it over and help them get over the embarrassment.
[Commentary] A very useful comment by Hugh, but not one that the counselor wants to reinforce until he sees how it plays with the rest of the group.

Karen:
38. Yet, if we made them stay when they didn't want to, it would restrict them too much.

Beth:
39. I think if someone is really embarrassed, and they just want to get away for a while, that's fine.

Sonstegard:
40. So we may not encourage leaving, but if people feel they absolutely need to, they have the right. (Pause) Now what if a person feels that he or she is getting nothing from the group sessions: Should people be forced to stay?
[Commentary] The counselor's inquiry about members withdrawing from the group follows naturally from the previous group decision and suggests a possibility the leader has encountered before.

Erv, Karen, and Beth (at once):
41. No!

Sonstegard:
42. What will they be permitted to do?

Erv:
43. Quit. If it's not doing them any good ...

Beth:
44. Well after all, the group is a volunteer thing anyway, isn't it? I don't think people should have to stay if they don't want to.

Group members:
45. Yeah, all right.

Sonstegard:
46. How about if we get to talking about really personal things? We bring things out in the open and discuss them in the group: Do you think there would be any danger in that?

Hugh:
47. I think that would be a real good way to handle things. Like if you are having trouble at home, you could talk it out and feel you were among friends; and maybe someone would have an idea on how to handle stuff.

Sonstegard:
48. But supposing some members of the group discuss it with people outside of the group?
[Commentary] The process of coming to group understandings is far enough along that the counselor can raise the issue of confidentiality. It is one of the few issues the counselor might raise if the group members don't.

Karen:
49. That would be bad.

Sonstegard:
50. How are we going to safeguard [against] that?

Beth:
51. Just by taking a vow or something that we won't talk about it outside the group?

Sonstegard:
52. Do you think we could agree to keep our meetings confidential, meaning that we don't talk about things?

Karen:
53. Yeah, because if I talk, then I might think that others would.

Sonstegard:
54. But supposing people get the feeling that we're holding secret meetings.

[Commentary] There is a difference between secrecy and confidentiality. Delineating the difference is essential to maintaining support for most group counseling programs, especially in schools and other agencies where privacy is not a given.

Beth:
55. Well, if someone asks me, I could give a general topic.

Sonstegard:
56. If someone asks, then, we can say that we talked about such and such, but not that Karen said this or Erv said that. That would cause mischief. (Pause)
[Commentary] Confidentiality extends from the therapeutic imperative to keep clients safe and to do no harm. The leader defines what constitutes harm and what reasonable communication with people outside of the group is. This distinction (with secrecy) allows group members freedom within needed limits.

A PSYCHOLOGICAL INVESTIGATION WITHIN THE GROUP

Sonstegard:
57. Are these [agreements] enough of a guide to get us through for a while? (Heads nod) Okay, what should we talk about?
[Commentary] Even in the first session, it is important to at least initiate a group discussion with therapeutic potential. A first session that only establishes group guidelines does little to inspire member confidence in the group process. A reconsideration of group agreements is still possible in the future. For now, the group leader implements one of their decisions by asking the members what they would like to discuss.

Karen:
58. I know one thing that had been bugging me lately. I'm in the last semester of my senior year, and I feel like the whole last year is a waste of time. I'm not getting anything out of it.
[Commentary] Karen again assumes responsibility for initiation, for responding while others are silent. She speaks with conviction, however, as if what is true for her is true for all: The leader begins

to suspect that integrity is very important to Karen and that she wants to be taken seriously.

Sonstegard:
59. Could you be more specific ... give me some idea about this "waste of time" you are talking about?
[Commentary] What Karen has offered is a general description. The leader tries to bring it to life by seeking a specific example. Karen is not ready, however, to go much beyond her initial declaration.

Karen:
60. I just feel really apathetic about school, about everything.

Sonstegard:
61. Getting bored with the whole thing.

Karen:
62. Yeah.

Sonstegard:
63. Hugh, what is the thing that bugs you most?
[Commentary] Karen stays relatively general in her declaration of discontent. The leader moves on using the same language (i.e., "bugs you") that Karen has used, but in a line of investigation designed to encourage participation by other members and avoid a one-to-one dialogue with a single member.

Hugh:
64. You mean around school?

Sonstegard:
65. Well, anything.

Hugh:
66. I don't really know right off hand.

Sonstegard:
67. If I pushed you just a little bit and said "just one thing"?

Hugh:
68. This is my senior year too. It hasn't been fun. Teachers do their best, but it ain't helping.

    [Commentary] Earlier Karen chose to stay with the safety of a general description. She was careful not to reveal anything personal about herself. Hugh, too, is cautious. When pressed, he plays it safe, taking a noncommittal position.

Sonstegard:
69. Beth, what about you?

Beth:
70. I have one more year to go, and I want to make the best of it; but like Karen and Hugh said, it could be bad. Right now, I enjoy school, like all my teachers, but I don't know. I want to have fun my senior year.

    [Commentary] Beth is a careful observer. She does not have as strongly negative feelings about school as Karen and Hugh, but she is not interested in taking a different position. Her process is to discover the position taken by others and to accommodate, to fit in by going along. Hugh is somewhat the same, but he is not as protective of himself as Beth. The counselor might guess that Beth comes from a family with high expectations and standards.

Sonstegard:
71. Do you have anything that bothers you right now?

Beth:
72. I can't think of anything.

    [Commentary] Beth is not about to commit herself to anything at the moment.

Sonstegard:
73. Okay. Erv?

Erv:
74. Well, the thing that bugs me the most is people telling me what to do, when to do it, and how to do it. They keep piling jobs on me, it seems like.

    [Commentary] Erv is candid. He is direct and explicit as contrasted with those who have spoken before him. Why the difference?

Maybe it is just his style; maybe he feels he has less to lose; or perhaps something in his family background suggests that this is a way to proceed. Whatever the reason, his approach is essential to moving the group process along, and responding to him in a nonjudgmental manner is imperative.

Sonstegard:
75. Um huh.

Beth:
76. Why don't you just tell them "No!"

Erv:
77. Because you tell the old man "No," and he backhands you; so that's no good.

Sonstegard:
78. So you go ahead and do it.

Erv:
79. Yeah, usually. I do it slower, and I do it my way, but I usually do it.
[Commentary] Erv is a covert rebel—sometimes called a "silent rebel." He feels, probably accurately, that he is not in a position to rebel openly: The cost is too great. Erv's experience is that his father is not only punitive, but obsessive about it too. Erv feels he is up against a massive power, a complete authoritarian.

Sonstegard:
80. John?

John:
81. Well, my parents are getting to be a drag. That's my problem. It seems like all the time, when I go home, I get hassled by them. I don't know what to do about it. They say I have a negative attitude.
[Commentary] John continues in Erv's mode: He, too, is explicit and frank. He may have been influenced by Erv or by sensing that he could share something of himself without fear of reprisal. It may also just be his style. John's issue could have been pursued, and it would have been legitimate to have done so.

Sonstegard:
82. Anyone else experience somewhat the same situation?
[Commentary] In this instance, the counselor was interested in encouraging further participation by the more noncommittal members of the group (Karen, Hugh, and Beth).

Beth:
83. Yeah.

Sonstegard:
84. In what way?

Beth:
85. Name it.
[Commentary] Beth, after venturing into what appeared to be an identification with John and his relationship to his parents, very adroitly avoids committing herself to any serious discussion.

Hugh:
86. Every night after school, a bunch of guys and I go to have a cup of coffee. Well, actually it's about six o'clock till ten. Then I come home, and my parents ask me a bunch of questions. They don't understand that meeting that way helps me get through the day.

Karen:
87. They think you're lying or something. They want to know where you've been, how long you've been there, and who you saw there.
[Commentary] Even though Karen's statement is offered as an apparent affirmation of Hugh's position, it is important to remember that she is really telling a separate story, related to her own life. The same is true for the following statement (#88) by Erv.

Erv:
88. I think parents are afraid of being embarrassed by you going into the wrong places.

Karen:
89. Yeah.

Adlerian Group Counseling and Therapy: Step by Step 31

Sonstegard:
90. You believe they're thinking more of themselves.
    [Commentary] This is a selective reflection in which the counselor draws upon Erv's statement to indicate that even parents have purposes to their actions that can be discovered and understood.

Erv:
91. Yeah, really.

Beth:
92. Sometimes I feel that I'm my parents' daughter and not a different person. I don't feel they give me a chance to separate from what they are.
    [Commentary] Beth's comment is a positive sign. She is beginning to feel freer and more confident even though she is not ready to pinpoint the real problem in her relationship with her parents. The leader's original decision—to divert the conversation from John's specific concern so that other members might offer their observations—seems to have drained off some of the group's apprehensiveness. A return to John's concern is now appropriate and may be more productive.

Sonstegard:
93. Now how long ago, John, did this whole thing begin with you? The feeling that you had a negative attitude.
    [Commentary] The counselor decides to focus on John's relationship with his parents; maybe the group can help him understand his interactive process. Adlerians have always had this systemic approach to psychological inquiry. Both John and his parents are in the relationship. Each contributes something to the process; any one of them could decide to change and, by so doing, interrupt or even end the conflict.

John:
94. It's just been mounting up this year. I'm a junior this year, and I'm active in dramatics. Doesn't seem like I'm home that much. I'm gone a lot. Home to eat and sleep, mainly. But anyway, they get on my back about it. And I don't see why; I'm doing okay in school.
    [Commentary] Here are the hypotheses the counselor is forming about John as he talks. (A) John is a junior. Unlike Karen and

Hugh, John cannot yet see the light at the end of the tunnel. He has also not quite given up on the hope that things can get better. (B) John is active in dramatics. This should be a good outlet for John; it's of a creative nature: He can be uninhibited, he can imagine, and there are few restrictions. Perhaps the dramatics teacher (coach) is more encouraging than other teachers and shows more appreciation for John's talents. (C) The parents' response to John's behavior, if reported accurately, indicates that they are becoming upset, fearful, and even angry. They may believe that they are losing control and that John could get out of hand. They probably feel their authority is eroding, and like most parents, this conviction makes them jittery.

Sonstegard:
 95. How many brothers and sisters do you have, John?
 [Commentary] Adlerians might introduce an investigation of birth order and family constellation at many different points in the group process. It is particularly useful when a member is talking about family matters, and the counselor is seeking to develop a clear picture of the pattern of coping the person has formed.

John:
 96. I have one brother and one sister.

Sonstegard:
 97. Who is the eldest?

John:
 98. I am. I'm sixteen. I have a sister, twelve, and a brother, ten.

Sonstegard:
 99. Now, how do your parents deal with your brother and sister?
 [Commentary] Adlerians seek to understand family constellation idiosyncratically from the perspective of each individual: It is not the birth order itself that counts, but rather the interpretation the person gives it.

John:
 100. They seem to do better with them. Seems like I'm the black sheep of the family. They understand them better.

I'm always doing things they don't like, and they take it out on me. That's the way I feel. Seems weird to be just saying that, but it's true.

[Commentary] John was 4 years old when his sister was born. He undoubtedly felt that he had lost his favored position in the family. Perhaps the parents yearned for a girl or favored the new baby girl in some other way. Whether there was gender partiality or not, the parents were then obviously busy with the newborn, a child who needed constant vigilance.

John has always had some interest in the attention of others. Even as a teenager, his interest in dramatics places him on a stage where positive attention is possible. When his sister arrived, John may have attempted to recapture the favored child position by the usual antics children use to keep mom or dad busy with them. Before the new arrival, this did not pose much of a problem. Now, it is different. The parents may seem constantly occupied with his sister, feeding her, bathing her, playing with her. It can be surmised that John tried hardest to involve his parents with him when they were at the busiest. His persistent endeavors may have driven a harried parent to lose his or her temper, even to punish the eldest, thereby confirming his loss of status in the family.

To add insult to injury, these same parents have a third child just as John is starting school. These siblings also struggle to find their place in the family constellation. They will be quick to sense that the parents disapprove of John's behavior, so each child adopts behaviors that are more acceptable to mom and dad. And at least one of the two becomes an expert at pointing out to mom and dad all of the misbehaviors in which John engages.

As John gets older, he comes to believe that there is no hope of winning over his parents. He avoids their disapproval by regularly staying away from home. He hangs out with friends who appreciate him and give a sense of belonging. If it turns out that his parents disapprove of his friends, so much the better.

Sonstegard (to the group):
101. Do you have any idea why they [the parents] may be on John all the time?

[Commentary] In a later session, the leader might pursue any or all of the above as a possibility with John; in an initial session, however, such discoveries should come from the group itself.

Beth:
102. Well, okay, they say John's the oldest. He's the one who should set the example for the younger ones. If they follow him, they'll be black sheep too and ruin the family name or whatever.

Erv:
103. You said it. I think that's it on the button.

Sonstegard:
104. Do you think people expect more of oldest children in the family?

[Commentary] This question extends naturally from the previous comments, but it is also designed to lead into a possible discussion on the impact of birth order, which might offer John some insight into his situation.

Hugh:
105. Not in my family. I have an older brother. He's twenty. When he was a senior, he'd go out and drink and things. They took it much better from him. Now I can't go out. I have to take care of everything. It's really a pain.

[Commentary] Hugh's comment demonstrates the significance of interpretation. He describes a family constellation similar to John's: Both families have an oldest, male child who is disruptive. As the oldest, John believes he is a black sheep with the younger ones favored. Hugh has the vantage point of a second child who believes the older one is favored, because in his family the oldest gets away with so much. Hugh really has no sense of how much his parents suffered through his brother's behavior, but the proof of their suffering is in the restrictions they place on Hugh. In the group, Hugh's declaration derails any attempt at using birth order to help John gain some insight. Another road must be sought.

Sonstegard:
106. Now what do you do, John, when they [the parents] get on you?

[Commentary] Real experience is always specific: Life happens in the details of everyday activity. The group leader senses that at least some group members are ready to share the details that might make a difference in their lives.

John:
  107. I just don't talk to them.

Sonstegard:
  108. Stay out of it. Stay away from home as much as possible.

John:
  109. Yeah, leave. Or I go down to my room and listen to my stereo.

Sonstegard:
  110. Get into some activity. (Pause) Now, how do you handle it, Hugh?
     [Commentary] The counselor leaves his inquiries of John for the moment to see if there are other members who might contribute to a group understanding. The comments that Hugh makes will shortly lead to more useful contributions by others.

Hugh:
  111. If they start yelling at me or something, I just sit there and tell them not to be so childish. And then I casually walk over and watch TV and ignore them.

Sonstegard:
  112. That helps?
     [Commentary] This mild confrontation works because of the nonjudgmental relationship the counselor has already established. This same intervention a half hour earlier could have put most of the group on the defensive.

Hugh:
  113. Well, it helps them realize that they don't have much to scream at me for. Half the time, they don't have any grounds.

Sonstegard:
  114. Why do you suppose parents do this?
     [Commentary] The counselor invites the group into a discussion of purpose. Such discussions are possible even with young children and are essential with adolescents and young adults. The goal of these discussions is to replace criticism and hurt with understand-

ing and humanization. If these young people can come to see their parents as human beings with hopes, dreams, worries, and imperfections, then their relationships with their parents are already changed.

Hugh:
115. Parents are trying to look after you. They're protecting the family name. There are times you wish you weren't related to them.
    [Commentary] Hugh is beginning to be more insightful about the parent–child relationship; he indicates some understanding of the parents' side of the relationship and their viewpoint but they are still the enemy.

Sonstegard:
116. Do you suppose they're afraid of you?
    [Commentary] The counselor introduces a humanizing idea. He suggests a "soft" emotion (fear), one that is neither hostile nor aggressive.

Hugh:
117. Yeah.

Sonstegard:
118. What do you suppose that means?
    [Commentary] Here, the counselor seeks to make a difference "that makes a difference": It is important to stay with the inquiry into meaning and purpose so that a new understanding can register with as many as possible.

Hugh:
119. My dad's afraid that as soon as I turn of age, I'll move out. My mother says whenever I do that, I can't move back. They are trying to hold on to me too much. My brother is twenty, and he still lives at home. When he goes out, they try to tell him when to be in. They shouldn't be able to do that.

Sonstegard:
120. If you were parents of children [who were] your age, how would you handle it when they wanted to go out?

[Commentary] The counselor asks the members to think beyond the immediate to a time when they will be parents. This is another mild confrontation that can be made more explicit in the following manner:

Counselor: Do you think you will get married?
Teenager: I suppose so.
Counselor: Do you think you will have some children?
Teenager: Probably.
Counselor: What are you going to do when your son or daughter behaves the way you do?

Hugh:
121. **I would be worse than my parents.**
(Group laughter)

Sonstegard:
122. **Worse, huh?**

Hugh:
123. **I worry a lot. I really worry about everything.**
[Commentary] The worry that Hugh verbalizes should be explored; it is something that other members of the group will share and will be able to handle. The counselor, however, has started a line of inquiry related to John and his relationship with his parents: Completing this investigation is more important to group process than addressing Hugh's worries. The counselor makes a mental note of Hugh's concerns so that he may return to them later.

Sonstegard:
124. **Do you think John's parents are concerned that he may not turn out right?**
(Group laughter)

Erv:
125. **I think they *know* he is not.**
[Commentary] Erv's comment is made humorously, and John does not seem to mind: He even joins in the laughter. Erv could dare to respond in this manner, because of the unexpressed camaraderie that exists between the two. The other members would not have attempted it, because it would have been construed as a put-down.

Sonstegard:
126. Now, why would that worry them?

Karen:
127. Well, because they love him, and they want to see him turn out to be a nice boy. But I think parents ought to give you a chance to grow before you move out. Like, when I get into an argument with my parents, I say, "I'm almost eighteen, and I am going to be out on my own. I need to learn some responsibility sometime." And they say that, well, when you're eighteen, you can go out and do what you want. But as long as you live in my house, you'll live by my rules. And I think that while you're living at home, you should be trusted.

[Commentary] Karen offers a relatively detailed and revealing position when compared to earlier contributions. She starts with a conviction that suggests parents actually love their children and want them to turn out well: This is a value that extends from her own life in some way. Next, she shares with the group what "bugs" her about her home life—the lack of trust she feels from her parents and her strong reaction to their rules and their attempts to control her. It is a contribution to the group that deserves acknowledgment.

Sonstegard (to the group):
128. Do you think it's a matter of "while you're living at home, you'll live by my rules"? Do you think that's the real reason?

Beth:
129. I don't think that's fair. I don't like that. Each person's different. You can't learn everything at home. If you want to go away for a few months, and they trust you, I think you should be able to go.

*[Commentary] Karen's reference to **trust** strikes a chord with Beth. She, too, indicates an issue that is bothering her in relation to her parents: a desire to be allowed some freedom away from home.*

Sonstegard:
130. What do you think about Karen at eighteen? Suppose she still lives at home. Do you think her parents will be as strict then as they are now?

[Commentary] Staying with Karen and the position she offers allows the counselor to both treat her concerns seriously and to accentuate the power of group problem solving.

Hugh:
131. I think so. Maybe even worse.

Karen:
132. I definitely do. When my sister was in college, she still had to call and say, "Mom, I'm going out for a Coke," after school. I think that's ridiculous.

Beth:
133. Yeah, same for my sister.

Sonstegard:
134. What's the difference then—between living under the same roof and having to conform or moving out? What does moving out have to do with it?

Beth:
135. I guess they feel you'll have learned something by then.

Sonstegard:
136. And maybe they feel when you're eighteen, no one will hold them responsible for you. And if you do something, it doesn't mean "I'm a bad parent." Do you think parents are concerned about being bad parents?

Erv:
137. Yeah.

Beth:
138. Oh, yeah.

Sonstegard:
139. I have a feeling about John: that his parents are afraid he'll do something that'll indicate they're bad parents. And they can't stand that. What do you think about that, John?

[Commentary] This intervention is a bridge from the work with essentially Karen and Beth back to John.

John:

140. **Yeah, really, because sometimes I just do things to get them ticked off. I do it on purpose.**

    [Commentary] This is John's clearest statement of his central position; he is a rebel: He believes that no one gets to tell him what to do and get away with it.

Sonstegard:

141. **How about school? Do you get in arguments with teachers?**

    *[Commentary] The counselor's question is designed to see if John's position with his parents relates only to them or has become his part of his style of living—a **pattern** especially in relation to authorities. Adlerian counselors always try to discover and work with human patterns.*

John:

142. **Not that much.**

    [Commentary] "Not that much" may be true, but it also means "yes, sometimes."

Sonstegard:

143. **What were the situations? Can you tell us a little about it?**

    *[Commentary] The counselor asks about John's **sometimes** to build on his guess about John's stance as a rebel.*

John:

144. **Well, once in P. E., the coach told me to do something, and I didn't want to do it. It's kind of bucking the establishment, you know. I'm going against everybody's rules, and I don't want to conform. It might seem weird to you, but it's the way I've been going about it.**

    [Commentary] John raises his rebellion to a philosophical level, seeing himself as a crusader against the establishment. John is a rebel, but he is not a fool; at school, his rebellion is more covert and selective. He is not interested in getting into serious trouble. The power he uses is more often asserted at home where he wants to be the boss. He proves to people that they cannot control him;

he adopts an "I'll show you" attitude. Apparently, his parents do not know how to cope with him.

PSYCHOLOGICAL DISCLOSURE WITHIN THE GROUP

Sonstegard (to the group):
146. What purpose does he have in mind, provoking his parents? He blames them for being on his back, but still he provokes them. So what purpose would he have?
[Commentary] Adlerian counselors seek motivation modification, and this change starts with a disclosure and understanding of purpose.

Beth:
146. Maybe he just wants to prove to them he can do what he wants without getting in trouble.
[Commentary] Beth, the observer, understands part of it. She even correctly senses that John wants to avoid "getting in trouble."

Karen:
147. Maybe they want to punish him by harping at him, by telling him when to be in; so he gets back at them by not doing it.
[Commentary] Karen is really suggesting the motivation of revenge—getting even with parents for perceived punishment. Getting even is probably a stronger motivation for her than for John. John seeks to maintain power: Revenge for him would be a waste of time.

Sonstegard:
148. I have another idea about it. Would you like to hear what I think?
[Commentary] This is the beginning of the Dreikursian disclosure process; it is designed to be a respectful and nonoffensive confrontation. The counselor tells the group that he looks at the data differently. He invites the group members into the consideration by asking if they would like to hear what he thinks.

Karen:
149. Yeah.

Sonstegard:
150. I think John feels power is important, and he maneuvers his mom and dad into power struggles and defeats them. "I'm going to show you, by golly."
[Commentary] The pattern and goal is disclosed to John in words that most closely parallel the language he has already used.

John:
151. Yeah, that sounds right.
*[Commentary] Goal recognition: In younger children, this recognition might be accompanied by what Dreikurs (1947) calls a **recognition reflex**, a little smile or twinkling of the eyes as if the person has been caught with hands in the cookie jar. Such a recognition can also happen in teenagers and adults, but John's considered response also counts as a recognition at a more conscious level.*

Sonstegard:
152. You see, your whole concern is about how much power you have. You use it in school, but not too much. But maybe you are subtler in school. Do you always get your work done on time?
[Commentary] The counselor refines the initial goal disclosure to see if his hunch about covert rebellion at school is correct.

John:
153. No.

Sonstegard:
154. Can you give us some instances?

John:
155. Well, I'll use drama. I'm almost always there. It's like a second home. They'll give us some lines to memorize, and I'll put it off until the last minute. Then I won't do it as well. I'm kind of a procrastinator.
[Commentary] John makes two important observations here: Drama is "like a second home" to him, and he procrastinates even in an activity in which he has a great interest.

Sonstegard:
156. Why are you a procrastinator? Does it not fit the same pattern we've been talking about? Nobody is going to tell you when to get things done. (Laughter) It's a subtle way of showing power in school.

*[Commentary] For many people, procrastination serves the purpose of avoiding anticipated failure; by putting things off until the last minute, one either believes that he or she "works well under pressure" or simply "runs out of time," but one never fails. This may partially motivate John too. But John does not say, "*I *have lines to learn, and* I *procrastinate." He says, "***They'll*** *give us some lines to memorize, and I'll put it off until the last minute" (bold italics added). John frames the interaction as a covert rebellion.*

John:
157. Well, I never knew about that.

[Commentary] John's response could put the counselor off, but just because someone has never thought about something before does not mean they can't do so now.

Sonstegard:
158. What do you think about it?

John:
159. Well, I don't think about all that. I just do stuff, like at home, to get them ticked off. I don't care.

[Commentary] John's response is accurate: He doesn't think about what he does; he functions best nonconsciously, without awareness. Actually thinking about his actions would impede his movement toward his goal of power. John would like to keep the process nonconscious.

Sonstegard:
160. They do exactly what you want them to do.

[Commentary] The counselor presents the goal once again, a mild confrontation to John's determination to keep the process out of awareness.

John:
161. Yeah. (John smiles)

[Commentary] John's acknowledgment and smile are a recognition reflex.

Sonstegard:
   162. If they didn't, you'd be real unhappy about it.

Beth:
   163. Then you'd have to think of something else to do.

John:
   164. Sometimes when they get mad, I start laughing ... uncontrollably.
   [Commentary] Recognition of one's goal often leads to a freedom to express the essence of one's pattern. John gets great joy out of defeating his parents.

Sonstegard:
   165. Do you remember anything that happened to you when you were a little boy? Like, one day something happened ...
   *[Commentary] Adlerians use **early recollections** for many purposes (Clark, 2002; Olson, 1979); one of the most common is to confirm a guess and/or a disclosure that the counselor has made. This is the purpose of the leader's intervention with John.*

John:
   166. I was about ... five. They were always telling me what to do. You have to dress like this, go here, go there.
   *[Commentary] What John gives the counselor is really **a report**: something that happened many times over an extended period. While not as significant as an early recollection, John's report still reflects his basic stance toward life: No one gets to tell him what to do and get away with it.*

Sonstegard (to the group):
   167. You see, John is a rebel. He doesn't want to do anything people want him to do.

Erv:
   168. I think most people are rebels.

[Commentary] Erv is supportive of his friend, John. He also signals a willingness to interact with the counselor.

Sonstegard (to Erv):
169. Do you feel you are?
    [Commentary] Most comments in groups are both declarative and personal. It is worth checking to see if Erv is talking about himself as well as the rest of the world.

Erv:
170. Yeah. I despise anything my mom and dad want me to do. Most of the time I do it to keep from getting in too much trouble, but I do it my way. My way is right, and their way is wrong.
    [Commentary] Erv really separates his motivation from John's in his first sentence. Erv looks down on his parents, **despises** them, and feels that he is better than they are. His final declaration sums up his superiority: "My way is right, and their way is wrong."

Sonstegard:
171. Because you're so superior?
    [Commentary] This is a very direct goal disclosure. It works because it follows immediately upon Erv's declaration and because Erv is a fairly direct individual, himself, and can receive directness more easily.

Erv:
172. Of course.

Sonstegard:
173. But sometimes Erv gets into difficulty. Why does he have to display *he's right and they're wrong*?
    [Commentary] Awareness is only one step in the process of change. The leader seeks to bring the consequences of Erv's position into a wider consideration by his peers. That's the community in which Erv lives, and it is in this community in which his position will ultimately have meaning.

Karen:
174. It seems like that's the attitude our parents display too: "I'm older, and I know more."

[Commentary] *Karen's basic position on her parents hasn't changed: They are always to blame.*

Beth:
175. Yeah.

Sonstegard:
176. Do you think he got it from his parents?

John:
177. Yeah. I've got what I've got from my parents. I really do think that.
[Commentary] *John speaks of his actions as if they are a disease he caught from mom and dad.*

Hugh:
178. You pick it up from your parents or friends.

Sonstegard:
179. Well, why then don't you pick up some of the good things that they do, instead of all these other things that are useless? They must have some good features that you could adopt.
[Commentary] *In their adolescent world, none of these teens would ever question the position that parents are to blame for anything that goes wrong: This position is axiomatic. The counselor has won enough of their confidence that he can point out an incongruency in their position.*

John:
180. I sure can't think of any right now. (Laughter)

Sonstegard:
181. I'm curious about Erv and this feeling [that] he has to prove people are wrong, and he's right.
[Commentary] *A single word (superiority) does not sum up Erv's life. The group leader comes back to Erv's stated position to see if a greater understanding might be achieved.*

Beth:
182. He's like my brother, out to prove something.

Sonstegard (to Erv):
183. May I tell you what I think? (Erv nods) Erv, you see ... you are quite a bright boy, but you have some doubt about yourself. You are not sure you are as good as you want to be. So you go about reassuring yourself by proving others wrong. You feel so much better by comparison. What do you think about that?

[Commentary] Adler's (1957) fundamental assumption about human dialectics is that behind every declaration of superiority there are feelings of inferiority or inadequacy. Erv lives by the imperative of rightness. We can guess that he has been raised in an atmosphere that is highly critical, in which every mistake has been highlighted and perhaps punished. Needing to be right is always a compensation for feelings of doubt. The imperative of rightness also implies a standard that is external to the person; any measure of achievement must always be taken in relation to others. When feelings of doubt start to arise in Erv, he looks around to find someone else who is not measuring up; a parent is a convenient target.

Erv:
184. Sounds right to me. That's kind of what I feel when I'm doing it ... subconsciously. Consciously, I feel good.

Sonstegard:
185. Yes, it makes you feel you have a place.

Erv:
186. Yea, that's right.

REORIENTATION IN GROUP

Sonstegard (to the group):
187. Now, what do you think John could do about his situation?

*[Commentary] Awareness, of which **insight** is but one form, is not enough in and of itself. The counselor seeks to help the group put a new understanding into action. John's situation, if resolved, really helps every other group member with their home life.*

Beth:
188. Well, I don't think he should start doing what his parents tell him, because that would only frustrate him, but ...

John:
189. Well, I didn't plan on it anyway. (Laughter)

Sonstegard (to John):
190. Are you interested in doing anything about it or would you like to keep on fighting them?
[Commentary] The group leader should never proceed with a reorientation if the person or persons involved do not want to engage in the process. Moving ahead without permission only invites resistance.

John:
191. I don't like to fight them. But it does seem like they think they're always right, and I'm always wrong. And I just do stuff to get them ticked off and prove to them ...
[Commentary] John says that he does not like to fight. This is an important admission—and one that is almost always true of children in relation to their parents: These teens simply can't imagine a life any longer in which they would be free from the fight. The counselor will return to John's desire for peace shortly.

Sonstegard:
192. ... to prove to them you have power.

John:
193. Yeah, right. (Pause) Well, they have a little bit.

Sonstegard (smiling):
194. You have to give them some credit. Very magnanimous.

John:
195. I let them have a little.

Erv:
196. Otherwise, where would you eat and sleep.

John:
197. I like to be charitable.

Sonstegard:
198. But I think it bothers you a bit. You say you don't like to fight.

[Commentary] The counselor returns to John's declaration that he does not like to fight; it is in this exploration that the possibility for a change in relationship occurs.

John:
199. No, I don't.

Sonstegard:
200. But power is a means for you to have a place. You think, "If I am not powerful, then I'm nothing." (Turning to the group) And nobody can stand to be nothing. So he uses this maneuvering of parents—setting them up and then defeating them—to find a place. But it's a useless way of doing it. Would you agree that it's a useless process?
[Commentary] The group leader starts the reorientation with a restatement of the essential pattern in John's relationship with his parents. Then the counselor turns to the group members to complete his intervention. There are two reasons for redirecting his comments to the group: (a) He is signaling to the members that this problem is a group concern; (b) by talking to the group, John is no longer the center of focus, and he is free to just listen. Listening is a receptive mode, and in this mode, he is more likely to receive whatever his peers have to offer.

Karen:
201. Yeah, but if you don't do something, you get pushed into a corner.
[Commentary] Karen expresses her hopelessness. She is really acknowledging a double bind in which many teens feel caught.

Sonstegard:
202. In other words, you feel you should stick up for your rights. (Karen nods) Would anybody disagree with that?
[Commentary] The counselor reframes Karen's reactivity into a proactive stance. Reframing her position is an empowering intervention. To be reactive requires Karen to be on constant guard against what others might do to her. To stick up for her rights requires only that she discover within herself the resources necessary to make an effective stand.

Hugh:
203. You should stick up for your rights and everything, but your parents ... they have got certain things you should go along with. You've got to have respect for them.
[Commentary] Hugh does not have a deep understanding of what he is saying, but he is beginning to sense that his peers must take some responsibility for their relationship with their parents.

Sonstegard:
204. In other words, they have this [respect] coming to them.

Hugh:
205. You need to show them some respect; but the way John does it, I don't know. Maybe doing something for your parents now and then.
[Commentary] Hugh disagrees with John's mistaken ideas regarding the struggle with his parents, but he does so without being disagreeable. He seems to sense that setting out to change one's opponent will not ultimately be helpful.

Beth:
206. Having a "mom and dad" day.

Karen:
207. I don't think that just because you're a parent you naturally should get respect from your children. I think you should earn it. They expect me to earn it from them, and I want them to earn it from me.
[Commentary] Karen feels a great deal of hurt in relation to her parents—perhaps because she feels unfairly treated in general. In a later session, her feelings and concerns should be addressed.

Beth:
208. If parents don't respect kids, that isn't teaching kids respect.
*[Commentary] This is the second time (see response #206) that Beth has added a comment that seems to align her with the previous group member. The group leader begins to suspect that **pleasing** [another of Kfir's (1981) personality priorities] is essential to Beth's style. Again, this is an issue that will need to be addressed in a later session. Her need to belong by placating others may be a compensation for a fear of being rejected. Left unchecked,*

Adlerian Group Counseling and Therapy: Step by Step   51

Beth could suffer a loss of identity as well as the anxiety that comes from having too many people to please.

Sonstegard (to the group):
209. Now, Karen seems to think that sticking up for your rights is very important.
[Commentary] The counselor returns to Karen's position to reinforce a proactive stance in her. His comment acts as an invitation for her to give voice to the strength that is in her.

Karen:
210. Right. At our age, we feel we should have some responsibility. We're anxious to get out on our own without anybody telling us what to do. To have them telling us what to do, at our age—it makes you so mad you don't want to do anything. Almost everybody's down on teenagers. They think teenagers aren't good for anything. But we have ideas other people should hear. We're just fighting for the right to be heard.
*[Commentary] Karen correctly asserts that she cannot **be** personally responsible when she has other people telling her what to do; parental micromanagement robs all youngsters of the chance to handle their own affairs and gain responsibility. Karen feels insulted; it seems to be a matter of personal integrity for her. She believes she has a lot to say and that she should be heard. What is important to this group process is that her peers hear her and that her opinion be respected.*

Erv:
211. Adults have always been down on us.

Karen:
212. Yeah, but it's worse now. Everything bad in the papers is linked to teenagers.

Sonstegard:
213. Why do you think it's gotten worse now?

Karen:
214. Part of the reason is that teenagers are doing more things that you get in trouble for.

[Commentary] A first acknowledgment by Karen that maybe teenagers play some part in the stand-off with an adult world.

Sonstegard:
215. Yeah? Well, how did it come about that teenagers—and even children—are standing up for their rights and doing more to get them?

*[Commentary] The group leader, as a member of the adult world, attempts to validate Karen's beliefs and values by bringing a wider understanding of **social equality** (Dreikurs, 1971) into play.*

Erv:
216. I guess we're tired of being treated like pets: "Here's my dog, Erving." Sometimes, we're treated worse than pets. You got to feel that you are equal to them.

[Commentary] Erv in his own unique style defines social equality perfectly.

Sonstegard:
217. You see, this is something new. Never before did children think that they were equal to adults. And it frightens adults—your parents—because they don't know how to live with children as equals. Do you think they're having a difficult time?

Beth:
218. My parents have always been the authority, had all the responsibility, and they don't know what to do otherwise.

Sonstegard:
219. What could be done to help the situation?

Hugh:
220. When the person becomes a father, he should treat that little baby as an individual right from the beginning.

Beth:
221. Sometimes I go into the living room and say, "I have something to say, and I need you to turn off the TV and listen." And usually they do.

[Commentary] Beth suggests an approach she has found effective in her relationship with her parents. In relating her method, she helps others to consider the possibility in their parent–teen relationships. Her recommendation is more effective because it comes from a peer as opposed to a professional counselor. If it works for her, perhaps it will work for others.

Sonstegard:
222. Do you think John could do the same thing?

Beth:
223. He could try.

Sonstegard:
224. It worked with you. Nothing works perfectly all the time, but maybe it's worth a try. (Pause) What else might John do? (Pause)
[Commentary] The counselor highlights the usefulness of Beth's suggestion and notes that nothing works perfectly. There is no need for others to get discouraged if the suggestion doesn't go as well as it does at Beth's house.

Hugh:
225. Well, maybe if John begins to feel he has a place just because of the person he is—and he doesn't have to have power to feel important—maybe this will help.
[Commentary] Hugh reiterates what he understands to be one of John's primary motivations, and he enhances it with an interpretation of his own.

Sonstegard:
226. Anything else?

John:
227. Maybe if I do something for my parents every now and then, it wouldn't hurt.
[Commentary] John responds positively to the suggestions he has heard from the group. His comment stands in startling contrast to the previous pronouncements he has made regarding his parents. His change of heart is too much for a counselor to let pass without comment.

Sonstegard:
> 228. Yes. Sometimes, when parents feel a little more appreciated, they change a bit. This is the difficult thing to learn. If we want to change someone, we are the ones who have to change first. (Pause) Well, this seems like a natural place to stop for today. When do we meet next?

Erv:
> 229. I'd like to meet every day. School would be a lot easier to take if we had this to look forward to.

Hugh:
> 230. I agree.

SOME CONCLUDING REMARKS

Adlerian group counseling is a teleoanalytic process that can be roughly divided into four phases: forming a relationship, psychological investigation, psychological disclosure, and reorientation. The heart of the approach involves the discovery and disclosure of the patterns, goals, and purposes that make meaning out of the everyday experiences, behaviors, movements, and histories of the group members. Because the counselor engages in an interpretive process, she or he must be sensitive to the responses of group members. No group session is perfectly executed, and group leadership involves both risk and the *probability* of making mistakes. If a group member disagrees with a counselor's interpretation or disclosure, it could mean that the counselor is simply wrong. When this is the case, admitting it and returning to the process of psychological investigation is the only thing required.

Some disclosures are rejected, however, because the counselor is careless in wording the interpretation. Interpretations, to be effective, must reflect the contexts and language that make sense out of the client's thinking and experience. When this happens, the client feels that the counselor is on the same wavelength.

An example: A group of fifth-grade boys started to get out of hand after a classmate named Amy succeeded in provoking them. When the counselor inquired about what was happening, the boys all suggested that Amy did this all the time, and that they got in trouble, but she didn't. When the counselor asked the group, "Why do you suppose Amy does this?" no answer was forthcoming. The counselor ventured a disclosure worded in the following manner: "Could it be that Amy wants to show the boys up?"

Amy's response was an emphatic "No!" The cocounselor rephrased the interpretation in a manner that fit Amy's psychological stance: "I get the idea that Amy wants to show the boys that they are not so hot."

"That's right," Amy said. "They're not."

Several interventions in the group counseling session just shown might have been worded differently and more effectively. Still, the group members gradually became more involved with the process, and in the end, a number of the members seemed to receive the help that was offered quite gratefully. John and Erv both gained some understanding of the motivations behind their interactions. Karen and Hugh gained stronger voices in the group process, and together with Beth, they offered ideas and options that made change probable. Indeed, the process of group members helping each other led to an integration of new possibilities that would have been lost in an individual session.

SUMMARY

In this chapter, we presented an actual group counseling session with a group of adolescents. In this session, we demonstrated our process for forming a relationship, including the establishment of agreements with group members. We also demonstrated the process we use to conduct a psychological investigation in groups, as well as different ways in which psychological disclosure might be accomplished. We noted along the way the guesses and hypotheses that were formed as the group members made their contributions, and we also highlighted our rationale for the interventions that we made at various choice points. Because a tight focus was kept in the group, even a reorientation was executed before the group ended: It is this emphasis on a tight focus that makes Adlerian group counseling a brief therapeutic process.

REFERENCES

Adler, A. (1957). *Understanding human nature* (W. B. Wolfe, Trans.). New York: Premier Books. (Original work published 1927)
American Counseling Association. (1995). *ACA codes of ethics and standards of practice*. Alexandria, VA: author.

Association for Specialists in Group Work. (1989). ASGW ethical guidelines for group counselors. *Journal for Specialists in Group Work, 15*(2), 119–126.

Clark, A. J. (2002). *Early recollections: Theory and practice in counseling and psychotherapy.* New York: Brunner-Routledge.

Dreikurs, R. (1967). *Psychodynamics, psychotherapy, and counseling: Collected papers.* Chicago: Alfred Adler Institute.

Dreikurs, R. (1971). *Social equality: The challenge of today.* Chicago: Henry Regnery. (Original work published 1961)

Dreikurs, R., & Sonstegard, M. A. (1968). Rationale of group counseling. In D. Dinkmeyer (Ed.), *Guidance and counseling in the elementary school: Readings in theory and practice* (pp. 278–287). New York: Holt, Rinehart, & Winston.

Kfir, N. (1981). Impasse/priority therapy. In R. J. Corsini (Ed.), *Handbook of innovative psychotherapies* (pp. 401–415). New York: Wiley.

Olson, H. A. (1979). *Early recollections: Their use in diagnosis and psychotherapy.* Springfield, IL: Charles C Thomas.

Sonstegard, M. A., Dreikurs, R., & Bitter, J. R. (1982). The teleoanalytic group counseling approach. In G. Gazda (Ed.), *Basic approaches to group psychotherapy and group counseling* (3rd ed., pp. 507–551). Springfield, IL: Charles C Thomas.

NOTE

1. The typescript of this session, alone without commentary, is an edited transcript of a tape made of an actual session in Pocatello, ID. The names of the group members have been changed to provide anonymity.

Part II

Theoretical Foundations

CHAPTER 3

Theory, Process, and Structure in Adlerian Group Work

In this chapter, we:

- Provide a flow chart outlining the structure and process of Adlerian group counseling and psychotherapy.
- Define the theory that supports the process and interventions used by Adlerian group counselors and therapists.
- Consider practical applications of the following Adlerian concepts:
  - Meeting group members and establishing agreements.
  - Psychological investigations and the subjective interview.
  - Recognition of purpose and patterns in the lives of group members
  - Uses of "The Question."
  - Family constellation.
  - Life tasks.
  - Early recollections.
  - Psychological disclosure.
  - Reorientation and re-education.
  - Group problem solving.
  - The generation of new possibilities, support, and encouragement.

Because Adlerians believe that all human problems are essentially social and interactive in nature, group approaches are and have been central to the development of this model. Starting as "Adlerian collective therapy" in the early 1920s, Adlerian groups can claim a long and diverse history (Corsini, 1955; Dreikurs, 1959). Hoffman (1994) describes the group methods that Adler used to work with children, teachers, and families in his child guidance clinics in Vienna, starting in 1921. Rudolf Dreikurs (1960) may also have been the first to use group psychotherapy in private practice, starting in 1928 (Terner & Pew, 1978). Both of these Adlerian pioneers developed and used group methods in an effort to reach a greater number of people in a shorter period of time. In this sense, Adlerian group therapy has always been a brief therapy approach. For the past 50 years, this brief therapy approach has been used in schools, community agencies, hospitals, family education centers, and private practice (Sonstegard, Bitter, Pelonis-Peneros, & Nicoll, 2001).

> Adlerian brief therapists bring focus to the change process, often using each session as though it is the only session they have to make a difference. There are two foci that guide every session. The first seeks to develop a systemic and holistic understanding of the people involved in treatment, including their rules of interaction. The second seeks to understand the goals the [clients have] in seeking help. (Bitter, Christensen, Hawes, & Nicoll, 1998, p. 96)

In this chapter, we present a step-by-step guide for the conduct of Adlerian group counseling and therapy. Although no group session follows this model exactly, the basic constructs associated with the process, structure and flow of group therapy are all covered. Using a flow chart (see Fig. 3.1) that we developed for group leaders-in-training, we delineate group process from group formation and psychological investigation through psychological disclosure to reorientation, specifying techniques for assessments and interventions that both address individual needs and group development.

Human beings are both hermeneutical and teleological. It is the human necessity for interpretation and reflection that creates meaning and self-understanding in life. It is not our past that determines who we are. Rather, we determine what our past has been, what it means, and to what extent it will be the context for our present and future. Further, it is *the future we intend or fear* that motivates us, that unifies

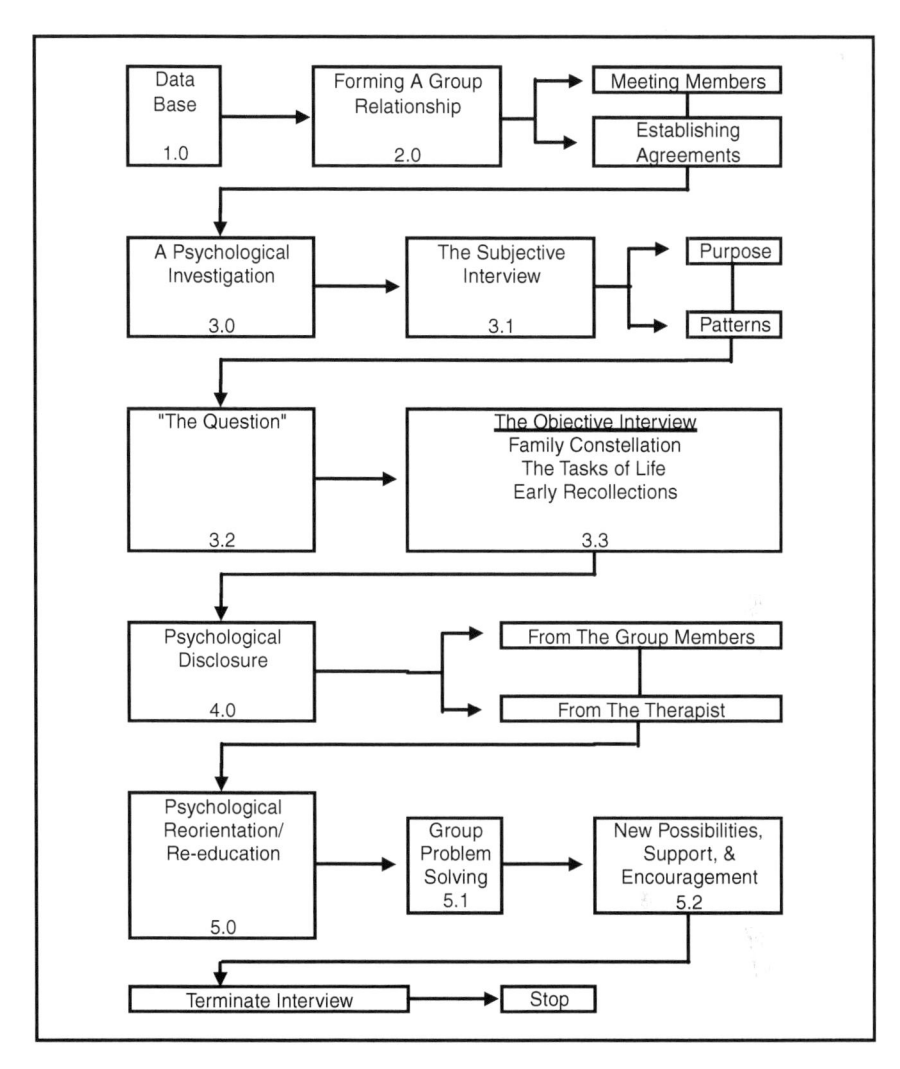

Theory, Process, and Structure in Adlerian Group Work 61

Figure 3.1

our actions, movements, and approaches to life. Adlerians believe that every thought, feeling, value, conviction, and behavior are in line with our central goals, the purposes we intend for our lives (Ansbacher & Ansbacher, 1956).

There are certain life tasks that are universal in life, challenging all humans regardless of gender, culture, age, race, or ethnicity. Adlerians identify these life tasks as (a) forming *community and friendships* with others; (b) making good use of our time in life by making a contribution—often through *work or occupation*; (c) finding love, creating *intimacy*, and in some cases, extending the family; (d) *getting along with oneself*; (e) *kinkeeping*; and (f) *spirituality* or connecting to that which is greater than ourselves (Adler, 1927/1957; Dreikurs & Mosak, 1967; Mosak & Dreikurs, 1967). We also join with Adlerians, such as Rachel Shifron (2003) and Peggy Pelonis (2002), in believing that *coping with the necessity of change* is a universal life task. People who do not feel up to these universal tasks of life often *retreat* from perceived group and societal demands into neuroses, depression, anxiety, behavioral disorders, and even the psychoses (Adler, 1935/1996).

Human mental health, on the other hand, finds both its foundation and its salvation in a movement toward others. Adlerians believe that people simply do better when they have a sense of belonging, are less self-absorbed, and have friends and family to whom they make a contribution and with whom they feel needed, valued, and important. Such people have what Adler called a "community feeling" (*gemeinschaftsgefuehl*) and the "social interest" that extends from that feeling (Ansbacher, 1992). Such people approach life with optimism, courage, and often a sense of humor.

Nothing tests a person's community feeling/social interest more than group process and group dynamics. People can take any position that suits their purposes in the one-to-one interactions that constitute individual therapy. In groups, however, all of the demands of life are reconstituted. One's sense of well-being, one's interest in others, and one's preparedness for human contact and social connection are all challenged and ultimately demonstrated. In groups, most people interact, and their interactions reveal their confidence or hesitations, their courage or retreat, their willingness to take reasonable risks, and their needs for safety. People both discover and create who they are in groups. Life's problems are enacted in groups. And except for the most severely disoriented clients, group therapy provides the treatment modality that most parallels human life.

ADLERIAN GROUP THERAPY: PROCESS AND STRUCTURE

Our model for group counseling and therapy is presented in Fig. 3.1, which is a guide and summary tool for therapists-in-training. Adlerian group counseling and therapy is an integration of Adlerian psychology with socially constructed, systemic, and brief approaches based on the holistic approach developed by Rudolf Dreikurs (1960, 1997).

Creating a Database

Information about clients and potential group members is often available to group practitioners, through either intake processes, referrals, or pregroup meetings when they are used. An early database can often help a group therapist to form initial guesses about the group, hypotheses that will later be confirmed or discarded. These initial hypotheses, to be useful, require at least some initial data that are psychologically relevant: *where* the person fits in her or his family constellation; *how* the person describes their personal concerns; a *description* of strengths and weaknesses, or *what* the person hopes to get out of the group experience. Adler was a master at constructing an initial assessment from data gathered by others (see Adler, 1970, "The Case of Mrs. A"). His hypotheses were often so accurate that an initial meeting with clients immediately confirmed his guesses. Whether confirmed or discarded, however, the act of engaging in an early assessment orients the therapist psychologically.

Although the *prescreening* of group members is common today (and even a requirement in some professional codes; e.g., ACA, 1995; ASGW, 1989), Adlerians, as we have already noted, typically reject this procedure. Although we have no objection to pregroup meetings that provide potential group members with information about group process and dynamics and help them to establish goals for the experience, prescreening is too often used to eliminate from groups the very people who could most benefit from the experience (i.e., those who are disruptive, self-absorbed, or isolated).

Even if a member of a group were to experience an active episode of psychosis—"hearing voices," for example—it is still possible for the group to both learn from the experience and provide the support needed for recovery. Similar to the investigations of the narrative therapist Michael White (2000), Adlerians would be interested in what meaning these voices have in the person's life, what purposes they intend for the individual, how the voices orient the person toward or away from others, and if the intentions of the voices are the goals that the person has for him or herself. These are all issues that can be addressed in a group and can help the person to recover a sense of value and belonging. Even if we knew a group member had the potential for a psychotic episode, most Adlerians would not want the person eliminated from group in a prescreening process. Indeed, we would prefer to work with the individual in a group of fellow human beings.

The reality of community mental health, whether residential or outpatient, and the controls of managed care usually negate the opportunities for prescreening of group members anyway. Groups are often formed as a part of ongoing treatment programs, and the members of these groups change intermittently with the flow of client populations. In many cases, initial data will barely provide the therapist with enough information to facilitate the integration of new members.

Forming a Group Relationship

For groups to get off to a smooth start, it is important for the group leader to address certain logistics, such as size, location, and balance of group members, which we address in more detail in the next chapter. Most of these issues require the therapist to reflect on what would constitute "optimal conditions" (see Yalom, 1995):

- With how many people can the therapist be fully engaged for an hour or more?
- Is there a location available that is private, free from distractions and noise, with good lighting?
- What balance of men and women, of age and culture, or of homogeneity versus heterogeneity is needed in the group?

Assuming these logistics can be adequately met, most group counseling and therapy sessions take place in a moderately comfortable setting with chairs placed in a circle. If group members begin to take their places before the session begins, it is not uncommon for some informal introductions to occur—and some early alliances may even start to form.

I (Jim) had the privilege of studying with the late pioneer of family therapy Virginia Satir (1983). She taught me that within everyone who is hurting or having difficulty with coping is a person who "would use himself or herself differently if he or she were in touch with the life that he or she is and has" (p. 246): especially if the person were able to tap all the potential that comes with an enhanced self-esteem. Like Satir, Adlerians believe that all people can be reached and that the avenues for touching people, although idiosyncratic, are all characterized by human contact, mutual respect, and a presence that includes interest in, care for, and faith in others. Satir (1983) believed that people could not keep from expressing the patterns and purposes that constitute and permeate their lives.

I am listening to their responses to me. In a few moments, I will hear responses from the people to each another [sic]. I begin to get a feeling for what they have done, how they have used their experiences from the time they popped out of the womb until now. (p. 247)

Meeting Members

Therapists must learn to begin *group process* with this kind of presence and interest in the people they meet, and they must learn to concurrently observe the group as a "process" entity. A number of questions facilitate such an observation:

- Who sits with whom?
- How do people enter and find a place in the group?
- Who talks to whom?
- What is the level of comfort or discomfort in the room?
- What kind of atmosphere seems to be present?
- What initial impressions are being formed?

When everyone is present, we catch everyone up on how the group was formed and any hopes or desires we have for the group process, and then we ask the group members to briefly introduce themselves. With children or adolescents, we often ask them to first meet in pairs, learn something about each other, and then bring the information back to the group. This process gives those who are perhaps struggling to find the "voice" they want to use in group a chance to practice in a dyad first.

> Counselor: I think I am the only one who knows everyone here. Each person here shares some hope for better contact with others, and it is my hope that this group will provide an avenue for realizing that goal. Why don't we start by picking a partner to interview so that you can introduce them to the group. You may want to tell each other your names and something you would like others in here to know about you.

By focusing on *relationship* from the very beginning, we are laying a foundation for cohesiveness and connection. Although these initial introductions are important, they do not have to take the entire session or even a major portion of it. Introductions are a chance for group members to break the ice and to use their voices, perhaps for the first time, in a group setting.

Establishing Agreements

When group members have had a chance to introduce each other, we generally ask them what *agreements* they would like to have in the group. As much as possible, Adlerians want group members to establish their own agreements for the group experience. As we have mentioned before, we do not use the concept of *group rules* or even *ground rules*, terms that suggest and too often reflect our authoritarian history and the superior/inferior relationships inherent in that history. Younger group members, especially adolescents, must feel that they have contributed to the development of the group process. Using material excerpted from the group counseling session in the previous chapter:

Counselor: We should probably come to some agreements before we get started. What agreements do we need? (A long pause)
Karen: Well, how often should we meet?
Counselor: How often do you think we should meet? How often would you like to meet?
Hugh: Wouldn't that depend on the problems we bring up? We might need to meet three times a week.
Counselor: (clarifying) Three times a week?
Hugh: Maybe.
John: I think three times a week is a little too much. Maybe once a week, maybe not that often.
Beth: I think if someone has a problem they want to talk about they should get in contact with the others, and we could talk then.
Counselor: (to Beth) How often do you think we should meet as a group?
Beth: As a group? Do you mean a regular planned meeting?
Counselor: Yes (nodding).
Beth: I think once a week would be enough.
Erv: We could have emergency meetings if we needed them.
Counselor: So once a week. Are all of you okay with that? (Pauses as he looks around at group members) Now, how long do you want each group session to last?

Although these decisions seem rather basic, they give some control over the group structure to the group members, and they lay the foundation for dealing with more important issues. Is the group open or closed? Can members come and go as they please or do they need to always be present? Can a group member choose to be silent, to observe, but not talk? What will the use and limitations of *confidentiality* be, and how will this essential concept be defined? Again, continuing with the same group:

Counselor: How about if we get to talking about really personal things? We bring them out in the open and discuss them in the group: Do you think there would be any danger in that?

Hugh: It might be a good idea, but I would have to feel safe in here, and I don't automatically.

Counselor: Well, suppose that some members of the group discuss what you say with people outside of the group.

Karen: That would be bad.

Counselor: What will be the safeguard against that?

Beth: Just take a vow or something that we won't talk about anything outside the group.

Counselor: Do vows work for you?

Beth: Not always.

Karen: It's hard though. If I can imagine myself talking outside the group—even a little, then I think that others would.

Beth: But if someone asks me something, my parents or friends or something, I could see telling people a general topic we discussed.

Erv: I could live with that.

Counselor: If someone asks then, we can say that we talked about such and such, but not that Karen said this or Erv said that. That last part would cause mischief, maybe even harm.

A Psychological Investigation

Adlerian psychological investigations focus on personal *patterns* and *motivations* expressed and enacted within the group and the social contexts experienced by individual group members. While most such investigations start with a *subjective interview* that allows group members to bring up various issues, Adlerians may introduce more objective inquiries, including *"The Question," family constellation and/or birth order, an evaluation of the tasks of life,* or *early recollections,* to name a few. These are discussed later in more detail.

Initially, what members choose to discuss in group sessions can be completely open. It is often enough to start by asking, "So what should we talk about?" With adolescents and younger children, we occasionally let the group members know the range of topics that have been discussed before: "I want you to know that I am open to discussing anything that is seriously important and relevant to you. In the past, groups have talked about family difficulties, sex, drugs, school problems, feeling hopeless or alienated ... anything, really." With adults, especially those hospitalized or in outpatient treatment, we note that we are willing to address specific concerns related to diagnosis, treatment, or therapy, but we are also there to work with the larger life issues and concerns that may present in their lives.

When group leaders open with such an invitation, they must be prepared to be tested on the integrity of their offer. Whatever topic is chosen, listening to each person's storyline, interaction processes, and group contributions will always reveal individual patterns and motivations.

The most common Adlerian interventions during an initial psychological investigation of the group include:

- Asking group members to provide the group with specific incidents to which the person attaches meaning.
- Asking group members to indicate how they feel in the midst of specific interactions.
- Watching the effect of individual contributions on the group as a whole.

A group member who complains that her parents are hopeless and that she can't talk to them opens an investigative door, but very little is known from the complaint itself. "When was the last time you tried to talk to your mom or dad and it didn't work out? How did that attempt go?" "What did they do, and what did you do?" Asking specific questions about "the last time" seeks to develop a narrative of the interactions embodied in her complaint. Her answers to these inquiries reveal her process and her perception of her parents' reactions; her answers may also suggest the start of a pattern *that she uses* in attempting to make contact with significant others. Further, the reaction of these significant others is often the very reason (purpose) for which the person initiated the pattern in the first place.

"And how were you feeling when this was going on?" The group leader gets to hear the reactions of the group member. More importantly, the emotional reaction will often provide a clue to the interpretations about self and others the person assigns to the event. If a pattern can be identified, it then becomes a guide for understanding possible interactions in the group itself.

The Subjective Interview

A subjective interview seeks to develop both *individual storylines* and *a group consensus* about what is relevant and important to most of the members. Finding a common language of inquiry often is a first step in this process. Karen may start by saying, "I know one thing that has been bugging me lately." What bothers her is important, but so is the language of "being bugged." The group leader will want to acknowledge what "bugs" Karen, and also bring the rest of the group along: "Karen says the attitude of teachers bugs her. What bugs the rest of you? Hugh, what bugs you?"

Balancing the development of individual storylines with the need for group interaction is critical. Finding or asking about commonalties that exist in the presentations of multiple members also helps to build a sense of *cohesiveness* in the group. Even if group members do not have similar life experiences, they can be asked to speculate about what meaning individual stories might have for the person telling it. What seems to matter to the person? What does it say about the storyteller? What goals or purposes seem to motivate the person?

Often group members will say things that seem on the surface to be contradictory. For example, in a group therapy session, a member we'll call Graham might note that he "tries to please," but he also "gets angry often and explodes." Adlerians treat such statements as *two points on a line*. In effect, we want to know how both of these statements can be true. What are the steps that get Graham to move from one position to the other, and what does this tell us about what motivates Graham? In this example, the steps might be: (a) Graham works hard to clean up the house, a surprise for his spouse when she returns; (b) Graham wants to be appreciated for his effort; (c) his spouse fails to notice or, worse, she point out the parts he didn't do so well; (d) Graham decides, "If she doesn't appreciate me for what I try to do, I will really give her something not to appreciate"; (e) at the next opportunity, he arranges to get angry at her and explodes. Understanding the purpose and pattern to this episode in the first step in interrupting a sequence that may very well be enacted without awareness, as if he has no control over his anger or what he does.

"The Question"

Adler (1927) used to ask his clients, "What would *you be like* if you were well?" Dreikurs (1997) adapted what came to be known in Adlerian circles as "The Question" in the following manner: "What would you be *doing* if you didn't have these symptoms or problems?" or "How would your life be different if you didn't have these symptoms or problems?" Dreikurs used "The Question" for differential diagnosis: When a group member said, "I would be doing better in school or have more friends if it were not for my anxiety," Dreikurs believed that the client was *using* the anxiety as an excuse for not succeeding or for lacking friends.

That is, the client was in full retreat from the anticipated failure that would presumably occur if she or he attempted to make a better life. In this sense, clients do not propose a desired outcome or solution to life's problems when they answer "The Question"; rather, their symptoms are their solutions—mistaken ones, to be sure—that help them to avoid life tasks and responsibilities that are perceived as necessary. Of course, it is possible that clients might answer that nothing would be different, except that the anxiety would be gone. In such cases, Dreikurs suspected that the pathology or symptoms were most likely organic, and he would refer the client for a medical evaluation. Let's look at how "The Question" might find a place in group work.

I (Jim) was once asked to consult with a parent "C" group (see Dinkmeyer & Carlson, 2001) composed of mothers and fathers who had already completed a basic parenting course. When the group members were introducing themselves, one of the parents, Jane, noted: "Ninety-three percent of my life with the children is going great. I guess I am here to work on the other seven percent." This is a fascinating introduction. There are a few questions that immediately come to mind: If that much is going well in her childrearing, what is she doing here? Shouldn't she be home writing a book? And why ninety-three percent? Why not ninety percent or ninety-five percent? Could it be that it is important to her to get things *just right*? This is an introduction that has *perfectionist* written all over it.

As the group progressed, members were asked to share successes, difficulties, and concerns. When Jane entered the discussion, she noted that the encouragement and logical consequences she used were mak-

Theory, Process, and Structure in Adlerian Group Work

ing a huge difference, but try as she might, she could not seem to get her youngest, a boy named Timmy, to stop interrupting her. After the group had offered a number of possibilities that Jane dismissed or said she had already tried, I asked her "The Question."

"What would you be doing with your life if Timmy were not interrupting you all the time?"

Jane replied: "I would finish the thank you notes I still owe people, because of my oldest daughter's wedding; I would finally get the attic cleaned out; and I would play the violin again."

I could understand the value of interrupting thank you notes and cleaning an attic. I even thought that maybe the first thank you note should go to Timmy for saving her from these tasks. But the violin?

"Tell me about playing the violin. Do you enjoy it?"

"Well, I haven't played in a long time, maybe twelve years really. When I was in college, I was a concert violinist: first chair."

Here, "The Question" reveals the value of the problem in her life. Timmy's interruptions keep her from engaging in tasks that she doesn't really want to do, and more importantly, they safeguard Jane from facing the fact that she no longer plays the violin *perfectly*, that she is no longer first chair.

The Objective Interview

Many Adlerian counselors and therapists will skip the objective interview when they have developed enough of an understanding of the people in the group from the subjective interview or through the use of "The Question." Still, the objective interview includes standard Adlerian assessment procedures that are very useful in group settings. These include an understanding of group members' *family constellations*, their personal approaches to the *life tasks* (especially Adler's [1927/1957] first three: friendship, occupation, and intimacy), or interpretations of each individual's *early recollections*. Some therapists use one or more of these assessment tools to confirm what they already suspect about member patterns and motivations. Some therapists, however, prefer a more intensive process called a *lifestyle assessment* (see Eckstein & Baruth, 1996; Powers & Griffith, 1987, 1986/1995, or Shulman & Mosak, 1988). Allowing for variations in style, it would be unusual for an Adlerian therapist to not introduce some aspect of this objective interview into one of the early sessions of the group.

In the group session in chapter 2; John was asked about his family constellation (his family system):

John: It's just been mounting up this year. I am a junior this year, and I'm active in dramatics. Doesn't seem like I'm home that much. I'm gone a lot. Home to eat and sleep mainly. But, anyway, they get on my back about it. And I don't see why; I'm doing okay in school.

Counselor: How many brothers and sisters do you have, John?

John: I have one brother and one sister.

Counselor: Who is the eldest?

John: I am. I'm sixteen. I have a sister, twelve, and a brother, ten.

Counselor: Now, how do your parents deal with your brother and sister?

John: They seem to do better with them. Seems like I am the black sheep of the family. They understand them better. I'm always doing things they don't like, and they take it out on me. That's the way I feel. Seems weird to just be saying that, but it's true.

From this limited information, Dr. Sonstegard is able to form an initial hypothesis about John's storyline. Developed as a narrative with a contextual beginning and a transition to John's current psychological stance, the storyline suggests the individualized personal meanings associated with John's interpretation of his development. Sonste guesses that:

> John was 4 years old when his sister was born. Perhaps he felt that he lost his favored position in the family with her birth. John has always had some interest in the attention of others. Even as a teenager, his interest in drama places him on a stage where positive attention is possible. When his sister was born and the family attention necessarily shifted to the newborn infant, John may have tried the usual antics that children use to keep mom or dad busy. Before his sister, this would not have been much of a problem; but after her birth, perhaps a harried parent loses his or her temper, even punishing John, the eldest, thereby confirming his loss of status in the family. To add insult to injury, the parents have a third child as John is starting school. The two siblings will be quick to sense the parents' disapproval of John's behavior, and each will adopt behaviors more acceptable to mom and dad. As John gets older, he comes to believe that there

is no hope of winning over his parents, so he stays away from them as much as possible.

John's *storyline* is a narrative of the psychological conclusions John has reached about his life. The counselor posits this tentative understanding based on an assessment of family constellation, the manner and mood in which John presents the data, and his style of interacting in the group. Considering the requirements of both tact and timing, the group leader might choose to use the information only as a guide for later interventions or, if appropriate, to present the narrative to the group as a tentative guess for group consideration. Appropriateness for the group process and John's openness to new information are essential considerations.

Family Constellation. An assessment of *family constellation* allows the therapist to identify:

- Major influences in the client's life.
- Interpretations the client generates about his or her position in the family.
- Experiences the person had with parents that set a guideline for gender identity.
- Interpretations of life and society provided by the parents.

Within this assessment, the client's phenomenological interpretation of *birth order* is primary, because across cultures, siblings tend to have a greater influence on personality development than parental involvement (McGoldrick, Watson, & Benton, 1999). Listening to each individual's sense of place in the family helps the counselor or therapist to understand the client's overall sense of place in the world.

Family constellation was Adler's (1927/1957) term for the family system. This system includes a number of significant subcategories, including the family atmosphere (within the parent–child subsystem); the family values (held and promoted within the parental subsystem); the gender guiding lines and relational model presented by the parents (as a spousal subsystem); and the influence of birth order (or process within the sibling subsystem). Each of these aspects of family constellation acts as an influence on the development of the individual. To be sure, the influence is considerable and powerful in personal lives. It is not the influence, however, that determines outcome: It is the individual's interpretation of these influences that counts.

Two people can grow up in a family atmosphere that is like a jungle where "survival of the fittest" seems to be the rule. One may attempt to be the strongest and most powerful by direct, overt action. The other may seek power through weakness: an attempt to gain advantage by declaring helplessness and the need for protection.

Similarly, two parents may hold a family value that promotes the importance of education. Maybe both parents are teachers and want their children to be among the most educated in their community. Although each child in the family will have to take a stand in relation to the family value, we will not know what that stand might be until we understand how each child interprets the demands placed on him or her and how the child evaluates his or her capabilities in relation to these demands.

Of all the influences within the family constellation, Adler (1931/1959) was most known for his phenomenological conceptualization of birth order and its effects. Adlerians see birth order as "a vantage point from which one views life. There are many possible ways to view life from a fixed vantage point; the only thing that a person cannot do is change the vantage point itself" (Bitter, Roberts, & Sonstegard, 2002, p. 44). Adler identified five birth positions that he delineated in some detail: *only, oldest, second of only two, middle,* and *youngest.* Although his descriptions of these positions often seemed concrete and fixed, he was really describing the probable influences that each vantage point held. It was still up to the individual to decide what she or he would do, given the position into which each person is born.

Only and oldest children share the experience of having parent(s) all to themselves. In the case of oldest children, this may be a short-lived experience. This commonality seems to account for a *high achievement drive* that the two positions share (Phillips & Phillips, 2000). Actual achievement may or may not follow from this shared drive, again depending on the individual's interpretation, but the drive is almost always there.

Only children are never dethroned. They develop adult language systems and competencies much sooner than other positions, and they tend to incorporate parental values. They seldom take a middle course: They may conform or rebel, but in both cases, they are reacting to the adults in their world. They may become pampered, overprotected, and spoiled, but they can also bask in the care, attention, and resources provided that lead to a high degree of success (Grunwald & McAbee, 1985).

Being first or being the biggest seem to be the most seductive influences on the eldest child position. It is as if they are born on top of a mountain and assume they are destined to be king or queen. Most oldest children are dependable, serious, responsible individuals with a tendency toward perfectionism. When their position is threatened, they can be sensitive, timid, or easily hurt. But mostly, they like to take charge, and younger siblings often describe them as "bossy."

The position of the second-of-only-two is largely influenced by the stance of the firstborn. Whatever position the firstborn assumes, the second is almost always the opposite in some fundamental way. This tends to be true even when the children are twins.[1] They may feel they are in a race, always trying to catch up.

Middle children feel squeezed between oldest and youngest children. They often declare that they are left out. To them, life is unfair: They get neither the privileges that come with being oldest nor the care and freedom that seem to come with being youngest. They may spend a great deal of time comparing where they stand to others. If they come up short in this comparison, it merely confirms life's unfairness. If the middle child complains a lot, the oldest and the youngest will tend to form an alliance complete with strategies that work against the middle child.

Like only children, youngest children will never be dethroned. Unlike only children, they are surrounded by other siblings. It is not uncommon for youngest children to become experts at putting others in their service. They play helpless and dependent in an effort to get others to take care of them. Youngest children are typically good observers, and they may use their observations to outshine all the rest of their siblings. They often want to be special, and with the right talents, they can be great entertainers.

We want to emphasize, again, that it is not the position into which one is born that counts, but rather the interpretation and meaning that are assigned to that position by individuals. For example, a sickly oldest child may easily fall into pampered helplessness as a means of securing service and care. A healthy second child may then assume the psychological birth position of the oldest. Or a middle child may discover that she can use a disease, such as anorexia, to demand care and service from others: In effect, she declares herself to be a better youngest than the actual youngest.

It is not uncommon in group counseling to ask the members to share some information about where they come in their families of origin. In a group therapy session with five young adults, Tami, Angela, Rebecca, Pat, and Chad, the birth positions look like this:

Oldest boy +7	*Angela*	*Rebecca*
Middle girl +5	Second girl −1	Second boy −3
Tami		Youngest boy −5

Pat and *Chad* are only children.

Keeping in mind that the interpretation is more important than the actual birth position, certain questions help us to gain a better understanding of these participants. For those with three or more in the family, asking "Which sibling is most different from you, and in what way" helps us to see the position from the person's point of view. Although we might expect Tami, for example, to be in an alliance with her oldest brother, it turns out that he was mean to her. He was also very much of a loner, and Tami's older sister assumed the position of oldest child in relation to Tami. "She [Tami's sister] always seemed to know what to do. I never do."

Angela is an oldest child with a baby sister the family calls "angel." It is not too hard to guess what the family thought about Angela's more dominating, bossy position in the family. "I was hard to get along with, I guess, but I knew what I wanted in life."

Rebecca is also an oldest child. She was asked another useful question: "Who was most like you and in what way?" She replied that she wasn't really like either of her brothers, but she favored the youngest. When asked why, she noted that he seemed to need her more. Rebecca and her next youngest brother were both successful, but in different areas of life. He was an athlete and a very good one. Both were good at school, but Rebecca excelled at art and music. She also found her place by being a caregiver, especially in relation to her youngest brother in a home with two very busy professional parents.

Pat and Chad are both only children. Pat, however, was raised by parents who stressed their love for her, came to all of her school activities and programs, and supported every dream she ever mentioned. Chad, on the other hand, was raised in a family where the atmosphere was tense, "like a jungle at night"; his father abused alcohol and Chad's mother. The few times that Chad tried to defend her, he was beaten. Their interpretations of what is possible in life, what to expect from others, and how to get along are very different.

In group counseling and therapy, an investigation of birth order and family constellation inevitably leads to personal stories that help all present to see each other in their unique contexts. When we know people's backgrounds and the stances taken in relation to those backgrounds, it is next to impossible to dismiss them and their needs. Their personal goals in group make more sense. Empathy and encouragement develop naturally.

Life Tasks. An assessment of *life tasks* allows the therapist to:

- Discover coping patterns that individuals use to handle life's problems.
- Look for areas of support and dysfunction in daily living.
- See the extent to which group behaviors manifest themselves in other parts of people's lives.

Friendship is really a social task that is essential for cooperative living. We have survived and continue to survive *as a community* in situations where we would never survive alone. How many friends a person has, what position he or she has with these friends, and what the person offers to and wants from friends all have a significant impact on quality of life: This task often helps to answer the questions we have about *who we are*. Occupation is really about how we use our time: what we do with our hours, days, months, and years of life. What do we do and toward what end? It includes the recognition that we cannot all do the same things and have a functional life. We must develop a division of labor and the capacity for contribution to cooperate in shared living. What contributions do we intend to make? When life is finished, *what will we be worth*? Intimacy has to do with what kind of closeness we want in our lives. It includes how well we get along with members of our own gender and the other gender: what it means to us to be a man or a woman. It is related to the contribution that we want to make in continuing human life beyond our own existence. We are a species, like most, that is made up of two genders. A minimum of cooperation between the two sexes is required just to birth and nurture the next generation. Although it has proven difficult over history, life demands that our two sexes learn to get along with each other. These were Adler's (1927/1957) original three life tasks.

Especially in group therapy, we ask about each person's handling of Adler's tasks of life. Who are your friends and what kind of life do you have in your community? From where do you get your friends? What do you do with them? What is your role with them? How would they describe you? What do you value about them, and what do they value about you? With regard to occupation, we ask: What constitutes your work, your activities, in life? What meaning does it have for you? How do you get along with colleagues, supervisors, and subordinates? Do you feel appreciated for your work? For the task of intimacy, we may ask: What are your love relationships like? Do you experience emotional closeness with chosen partners? Do you have any difficulty in expressing or receiving love and affection from others? How would you describe men and women? How do you feel about yourself as a man or woman? What do you complain about in your partner? What does your partner complain about in you? To each of these areas, we might ask the Powers and Griffith (1987) question, "What do you want to improve or change in this area of your life?" (p. 59); it is a question designed to elicit personal goals that may become part of the group process.

In the last half of the 20th century, Adlerians added at least three other life tasks to Adler's original list. They are self-care or getting along with oneself, kinkeeping, and spirituality (Bitter et al., 1998).

Dreikurs and Mosak (1967) added the task of self-care that they called "getting along with oneself." *Getting along with oneself* is a complicated notion, because Adlerians do not really believe that a person can be separated into parts: How can I stand back from myself as a separate entity and learn to get along with me? Still, people are capable of reflection and reflective assessments that lead to conclusions that either elevate or discourage.

In a very simple and not too consequential form, I might look up the block and see that my neighbor has a new sports car and I don't. I think my 1990 compact should be better than it is, and I feel bad by comparison. On the other hand, if I look down the block and I see a homeless person pushing all of his belongings in a grocery cart, I immediately feel better about my position in life—even thankful for the gifts I have, like that old 1990 compact car that still runs after all these years.

The tendency to *compare* oneself with others is a natural human process. It is the interpretations that we give to these reflective comparisons that determine whether we are able to *get along with ourselves* well. People who are self-critical, pessimistic, anxious, perfectionistic, guilt-ridden, or overly impressed with their imperfections and weaknesses tend to retreat from the task of getting along with oneself.

We also recognize that the care of children and the elderly is no longer—if it ever was—merely a task for a nuclear family. We all have a stake in how younger people are raised and how the elderly are treated. With luck, we will all be elderly one day. We will still want to count, to matter, to be useful, and we will depend on younger people, just at they may depend on us now, for support, care, and meaning. Kinkeeping, therefore, is part of the activities associated with social interest: It is our ability to extend care into other generations.

When we extend this care into the cosmos, into our collective histories and futures, then we are also meeting the task of placing our lives and actions in a greater context that many people now call, in the largest sense of the word, *spirituality* (Sweeney, 1998). This life task begins with the realization that we are, as individual humans, really very small parts of the universe. Yet we are connected to so many things that are greater than we are. Among these connections are history; the environment; humanity as a whole; life, loss, and death; and in some cases, religious or spiritual communities and the moral codes that emanate from community living (Mosak & Dreikurs, 1967). For Adlerians, the meaning of life is contribution. It is active and includes care for our world, an appreciation of diversity, and the necessity of social advocacy.

Here, we also add another universal task for consideration: the task of *coping with change* in life (Pelonis, 2002). Because change is often associated with stress and distress, it is commonly resisted (Selye, 1974). But life *is* change. Our friendships, work, intimate relationships, families, cultures, and communities: All are in a constant state of flux. What we perceive as growth and development is change. Those with social interest greet change as an opportunity and sometimes a challenge. It is a part of life. It is an adventure.

In groups, life tasks can be used as *area assessments* to see where group members are finding real meaning in their lives and where they feel life is coming up short for them. Because life tasks affect the whole human being throughout life, it is not uncommon for individual responses to life tasks to change over time—and hopefully to grow developmentally with the person. They test our preparation for living.

When we successfully meet these life tasks, we express an essential feeling of belonging. This feeling of belonging, of having a place with our fellow humans, mitigates the experience of fear, loneliness, and desperation. Our sense of belonging gives us courage—and in many cases, confidence—as we move toward our personal and collective goals in life. That most powerful sense of belonging is intimacy: It is the feeling that with at least one other person we are loved, valued, and safe. More than any other task, the feeling of intimacy requires a close relationship characterized by *social equality* (Dreikurs, 1946, 1971).

Any investigation of life tasks may elicit areas in which individuals respond with "yes," "yes, but," and, in the case of serious retreat, perhaps even "no." Most of us have some combination of "yes" and "yes, but." We face some of life's demands with relative ease, and we have other challenges that bring up feelings of inadequacy. Those who lack social interest are ill prepared for life and life's problems. When faced with a difficulty, they retreat into self-interest—or worse, self-absorption. They lose courage. Fear, anxiety, depression, and substance abuse, to name a few, are all manifestations of this neurotic retreat.

In none of these cases, however, will the advantage of social interest be disputed.

> In every case there is a "yes" that emphasizes the pressure of social interest, but this is invariably followed by a "but" that possesses greater strength and prevents the necessary increase in social interest. ... The difficulty of a cure is in proportion to the strength of the "but." This finds its strongest expression in suicide and in psychosis, following on shocks, when the "yes" almost disappears. (Adler as cited in Ansbacher & Ansbacher, 1956, pp. 156–157)

The traits that emanate from a feeling of belonging are cooperation, friendship, empathy, caring, interest in others, courage, and confidence. Our capacity for this community feeling is the measure of our mental health. People with social interest meet these tasks with a willingness to solve them usefully. They treat others as they would want to be treated. They contribute. They participate. They seek to make a difference. "Psychological tolerance depends on the strength of social ties" (Adler, 1923, p. 42).

Group counseling and therapy remind us that we are not alone, that we can be interested in the well-being of others and allow others to be interested in us. Social interest is augmented by group process. We find our own strength in the support of others.

Early Recollections. Adlerian therapists use *early recollections* for different purposes, including:

- An assessment of each person's convictions about self, others, life, and ethical stances.
- An assessment of members' stances in relation to the group process and the counseling relationship.
- Verification of coping patterns and motivations.
- An identification of strengths, assets, or interfering ideas or mistaken notions in each person's life.

Because Adlerians use early recollections as a projective technique (Mosak, 1958), we tend to introduce them with an open-ended request: "Think back to when you were very little, and tell me something that happened to you *one time*." Most people have between 6 and 12 early (age 8 or younger) memories; these memories are self-selected stories that the individual uses to maintain a sense of constancy about self and life (Adler, 1927/1957). The content in memories is not as important as "why" the client has them. The client's life position in the memory is often as revealing as is thinking about the memory as a story with a moral (a specific meaning). Interpretations are achieved collaboratively within groups. We ask group members to offer guesses about possible meanings. In the end, each person must agree with or recognize the interpretations that have personal meaning.

Adler (1930, 1938) noted that these early memories were self-selected, not by chance, but with purpose. In group, when we ask for early recollections, we generally want each participant to "think back to when they were much younger—sometime before the age of nine. Tell us something you remember that happened one time." We also want to know what age the person is at the time of the memory and what feeling or reaction the person had at the time of the experience. This approach is structured so that no harm is done to the projective quality of the recollection. We do not ask, for example, for a *favorite* memory or for something that happened many times. We do not prompt group members with suggestions of specific times ("when school started") or specific events ("any birthdays that come to mind"). We want each person to start with a blank slate and bring forth a memory that is unique to him or her.

Early recollections have been used effectively in counseling and therapy for almost 100 years. They have been employed in a variety of ways and settings (Clark, 2002). Early memories can be used to reveal personal stances, connect past events to present experience, and relieve the entrapment of difficult feelings. Early recollections can also be used to explore the relationship between the group members and the leader. They can be used to measure progress toward desired change and goals, especially when memories are requested at the beginning of a group process and again toward the end of the group.

Experience and practice are probably the best ways to reach a competent understanding of the meaning revealed in early recollections. It is not uncommon for us to ask counselors- and therapists-in-training to collect two to three hundred different recollections from as many as 25 to 30 people. This is generally a good start. It allows people to look at each memory as a whole: What meaning stands out? What conclusion would one draw from the memory? If this memory were a newspaper story, what would the headline be? It also allows people who are new to the process to consider the collected meaning or ideas that emerge when an individual presents six to twelve memories. Clark (2002) developed a very useful "early recollections interpretation worksheet" (p. 131) that helps therapists consider early memories from multiple perspectives, including what the memories reveal about self, others, and life-events.

We want to emphasize, however, that it is best to learn the interpretation of early memories in the larger context of a lifestyle assessment and under the supervision of a competent counselor or therapist. Usually, a single course or reading a book is not enough. Like all projective techniques, it is possible to do harm with misinterpretations or overly zealous presentations. Effective supervision, which we describe in chapter 6, is the best safeguard against the misinterpretations of early memories.

Returning to the group with Tami, Angela, Rebecca, Pat, and Chad, a sample of their recollections is as follows:

Tami: (Age 6.) I was invited to a girl's birthday party. She was in my class at school. She didn't like the gift I got her. She made fun of me in front of others. I didn't want to be there any longer. No one liked me.

(Age 7.) People in my neighborhood were choosing up sides for baseball. I was the youngest one there, and I had never played before, but I wanted to. No one would choose me. I was told I couldn't play and that I should go home.

Angela: (Age 1.) I can remember my sister coming home from the hospital with my mother. I can! She was little, and she was asleep. And I went up and kissed her, like a doll. I liked seeing her, but I didn't think she was going to stay. When I realized that, I wasn't so happy with her.

(Age 5.) It was to be my first day of school. I came down for breakfast, and my mother said I could have whatever I wanted. I said I wanted ice cream for breakfast, and she gave it to me. It was special. I loved that day.

Rebecca: (Age 4.) I have been outside playing in the summer sun. All I have on is my bathing suit bottoms, but I am really tan. I walk into my house where my mother is sitting with friends. She calls me over to pull my pants down just a little and show people how tan I am. I see them smiling and feel appreciated.

(Age 4.) I remember later that summer, my mother asked me if I wanted to go to school like the bigger kids in the neighborhood. I said I wanted to go to the big school up the block, but not the small school where my cousin went. The big school was a high school, and it has a nursery school in one room there. My mom said: "Fine." And we had an agreement.

Pat: (Age 7.) I learned to play the guitar, an old one of my father's. My uncle taught me a few chords and a song to go with it, and I could do it. I played it for my parents, and they watched me in amazement. I felt like a star. It was wonderful.

(Age 8.) My mother came to school with me. We had a spelling bee, and I won it in my classroom. I spelled a word from a fourth grade book. My mother was thrilled, and I was very, very happy.

Chad: (Age 6.) We had to get shots, vaccinations. Maybe it was for school, I'm not sure. Anyway, I got my shots and went home. A couple of neighborhood kids jumped me, and they were hitting me on my sore arm. They made it worse. Later, when I told my dad, he said: "What's the matter? Can't you take it?" Then, he hit me on my arm a couple of more times. I was scared of the kids, of my dad, of everyone, I guess. My arm hurt, but I didn't want anyone to see me cry. (Chad wouldn't report a second memory.)

Even a rather minimal interpretation of these memories helps us to understand the members of this group a little better. Tami's fear of rejection is dramatized in each of her memories; so is her desire to be a part of everything. Angela's memories suggest her desire to be special. When her sister is brought home from the hospital, she knows what to do to please adults, but the real message is in her change of attitude when she discovers that the baby is staying. She wants to be her mother's only child. What that might be like is highlighted in her second memory. Rebecca is also an oldest child, but she feels more at home in front of others—even when mildly exposed; she feels appreciated. She also wants a say in what happens to her, but she generally feels that life will work out and she will be valued. Pat is an only child. Like Rebecca, Pat is accomplished and used to center stage. Achievement is what counts for Pat. Chad, on the other hand, lives in a physical and psychological jungle. When he is down, he expects things to only get worse. His feeling about men is that they are hurtful and dangerous. He is a victim. If "real" men are tough, he is not one of them.

Psychological Disclosure

Psychological disclosures might happen at any point in the group process. Although initial disclosures tend to come from the group leader, it is important to involve group members in the process as soon as possible. The group is invited to investigate meaning in each other's lives as a foundation for working with each other and considering desired changes. Psychological disclosures are used to:

- Create understanding by making unconscious processes conscious.
- Confront useless interactions in the group.
- Explore possible motivations behind behaviors.

All behaviors, feelings, values, and convictions have a purpose that is social in nature. Understanding the social results of a member's behavior is the easiest way to discover goals and purposes. Disclosures often follow from any of the assessments that are part of the objective interview described earlier. Here is an example from another group session with the same adolescents from chapter 2:

Erv: I can't stand it when my dad tells me what to do. He really doesn't ever know what he's talking about, and he never listens to anybody else. I just love it when

Counselor: he messes up. Especially if I'm in a position to say I told you so.
Counselor: Erv, can you think back to when you were little? Do you remember something that happened one time?
Erv: Anything? (Counselor nods.) Well ... I was in the first grade, and this college student came to give me an intelligence test. He had to practice or something. And he wanted me to put this puzzle together, but even with the manual he couldn't do it himself. So I watched him struggle for a while, and I, like, figured out how to do it. So I took it from him and just did it. I sat back and felt great. I was smarter than he was.
Counselor: What do the rest of you think this might mean to Erv and how does it fit with what he has been talking about?

A number of different interpretations were offered by group members, but the one that seemed to fit best for Erv was also the most blunt and direct.

Karen: I think Erv feels he is better than most everyone else, and he always wants people to know that he is right and others are wrong. It's how he stays on top, the best.

Though strongly worded, Karen's interpretation made the most sense to Erv. He could almost immediately identify other events in which this meaning was present. Another reason Erv could accept Karen's interpretation is that it came in a tone of voice that contained no indication of criticism or negative judgment. In general, interpretations that come from group members tend to have more impact than those that are offered by counselors or therapists.

Had an Adlerian therapist decided to add a guess to the process, Dreikurs' (1961) formula for psychological disclosure would commonly be used:

- "Do you know why you (do, feel, behave) as you do?"
- "I have an idea. Would you like to hear it?"
- "Could it be that ...?"

Psychological disclosures offered tentatively, as guesses, invite collaboration within the group. In this sense, even incorrect guesses have value. They demonstrate that the therapist is willing to risk being wrong in an effort to understand. Further, the elimination of an incorrect guess often leads to a better interpretation and allows group members to experience mutual respect in the therapy process.

Psychological Reorientation and Reeducation

Psychological reorientation is about changing group members' stances in life. It is about helping people to cope and to approach life's tasks in a *useful* manner. Adlerians define this usefulness as:

- A sense of belonging and feeling valued in one's community.
- A movement away from self-absorption, withdrawal, isolation, or self-protection, toward the development of a community feeling and social interest.
- The enactment of traits commonly associated with a community feeling, such as courage, the acceptance of imperfection, confidence, a sense of humor, a willingness to contribute, an interest in the welfare of others, and a friendly approach to people (Ansbacher & Ansbacher, 1956; Bitter & West, 1979).

Sometimes psychological reorientation is accomplished through reframing, a modification of motivation, the creation of new meaning, or the development of new possibilities and options. The most common reorientation process in groups, however, is group problem solving.

Group Problem Solving

Successful group problem solving depends on and flows from having established a *psychological* understanding of self and other people involved in any problem.

Returning to John, a young man in the group in chapter 2 who either fights with his parents or stays away from home because he feels he has no place in his family, the counselor asks: "Now, what do you think John could do about his situation?"

Beth: Well, I don't think he should start doing what his parents tell him, because that would only frustrate him, but ...
John: Well, I didn't plan on it anyway. (laughter)

Counselor: Are you interested in doing anything about it or would you like to keep on fighting them?
John: I don't like to fight them. But it does seem like they think they're always right, and I'm always wrong. And I just do stuff to get them ticked off and prove to them ...
Counselor: ... to prove to them you have power.
John: Yeah, right. (Pause) Well, they have a little bit.
Counselor: (smiling) You have to give them some credit. Very magnanimous of you.
John: I let them have a little.
Erv: Otherwise, where would you eat or sleep.
John: I like to be charitable.
Counselor: But it bothers you a bit. You say you don't like to fight, but power is a means for you to have a place. You think, "If I am not powerful, then I am nothing." (Turning to the group) And nobody can stand to be nothing. So he uses this maneuvering of parents—setting them up and then defeating them—to find a place. But it's a useless way of doing it. Would you agree that it's a useless process?
Karen: Yeah, but if you don't do something you get pushed into a corner.
Counselor: In other words, you feel you should stick up for your rights. (Karen nods)
Hugh: I don't know. I think parents have some respect coming to them. You need to show them some respect, but the way John does it, I don't know. Maybe doing something for your parents now and then.
Karen: I don't think that just because you're a parent you naturally should get respect from your children. I think you should earn it. They expect me to earn it from them, and I want them to earn it from me.
Beth: If parents don't respect kids, that isn't teaching kids respect. My parents have always been the authority, had all the responsibility, and they don't know what to do otherwise.
Counselor: What could be done to help the situation?
Beth: Sometimes I go into the living room and say, "I have something to say, and I need you to turn off the TV and listen." And they usually do.

Counselor: Do you think John could do the same thing?
Beth: He could try.
Counselor: It worked with you. Nothing works perfectly all the time, but maybe it's worth a try. (Pause) What else might John do?
Hugh: Well, maybe if John begins to feel he has a place just because of the person he is—and he doesn't have to have power to feel important—maybe this will help.
Counselor: Anything else?
John: Maybe if I do something for my parents every now and then, it wouldn't hurt.
Counselor: Yes. Sometimes, when parents feel a little more appreciated, they change a bit. This is a difficult thing to learn. If we want to change someone, we are the ones who have to change first. (Pause) Well, this seems like a natural place to stop for today.

In this example, John's concern has been noted, and the group leader suggests the possibility that group members might be helpful seeking solutions. *Group problem solving* and the *generation of new possibilities* tend to go hand in hand. In a sense, the steps in group problem solving have been part of the group process from the beginning. They include:

- Establishing an atmosphere of safety and mutual respect.
- Clarifying a psychological understanding of the group member's interactions and pinpointing the real issues.
- Asking the group member if he or she is open to input from others.
- Generating as many options as possible.
- Identifying a constructive possibility that seems to fit for the client.

In the end, John indicates which of the possibilities suggested seems to fit for him: "Maybe if I do something for my parents every now and then, it wouldn't hurt." The enactment of new possibilities almost always requires *support* and *encouragement*. It is not uncommon for Adlerians to use role playing and other psychodramatic techniques to aid group members in the practice of proposed solutions (Corsini, 1966). Support and encouragement also come in the form of having a group of peers "standing in your corner" and "believing in you." Being part of a group also means that you never have to experience success alone. Counseling and therapy groups are ideal places in which to celebrate member successes.

Although most group sessions seem to arrive at a natural stopping point, it is one of the tasks of the group leader to be cognizant of time and to not generate new material or processes when it is close to the end of the session's work. Indeed, even though most groups are ongoing, Adlerians treat each group as an entity in itself; that is, the group process for the session may serve a goal or purpose, propose or complete some work for one or more group members, or facilitate a new learning or meaning. Summarizing the achievements of sessions lays the groundwork for the eventuality that the group itself will one day end.

Many groups are part of agency offerings that continue even with group members entering and leaving at irregular rates. Although it is not always possible, Adlerians seek to honor these "comings and goings" by noting changes in the group, introducing new members, and acknowledging the importance and loss of group members when they get ready to leave. Groups that have been formed for a given purpose are usually time limited. Such groups will need one to two sessions to reach closure, to value the experience, to complete any unfinished business, and to develop referrals and follow-up meetings for those who may still need help and support.

Some time-limited groups explore the possibility of meeting on a short-term basis again in 6 months or a year. This process allows the group members a formal way to check-in with each other and to further mark progress in their lives. When structured with formal follow-up meetings, Adlerian group psychotherapy may never officially terminate. It is merely "interrupted," a form of brief, intermittent therapy (Bitter & Nicoll, 2000, p. 38).

SUMMARY

In this chapter we have used a step-by-step flow chart to suggest a structure and flow to Adlerian group counseling and therapy. Along the way, we have integrated essential Adlerian theory in a manner designed to make sense out of the various choices and interventions that a counselor might make. A common Adlerian four-stage structure of *forming a relationship*, conducting a *psychological investigation*, using *psychological disclosure*, and *reorientation* and *reeducation* has been enlarged to more carefully delineate processes for meeting group members; establishing agreements; conducting a subjective interview with the goal of discovering purposes and patterns; using "The Question"; investigating the interpreted influences of family constellation, life tasks, and early recollections; and engaging the group in effective problem solving.

Perhaps the most important difference that group counseling and therapy makes is in helping group members to cope with change through generating new possibilities, offering support, and providing encouragement. The word encouragement literally means "to build courage," and it stands in direct opposition to discouragement. In general, Adlerians believe that courage is built from strengths, from a sense of "being a part of," and from getting in touch with both internal and external resources. Groups have great potential for providing all of these ingredients. Encouragement flows from the faith group members come to have in each other, from the hope that comes from group support, and from a communication of caring that often comes from both group members and the counselor or therapist. Properly tended, groups become what Miriam Polster (1999) called a "safe emergency" (p. 107), a place to try new possibilities and to consider new options. Groups invest social interaction with real meaning, because groups will not only help an individual member, but will also evoke in that member a desire to help others. As we have noted before, when a group member offers help to another member, we immediately know two things: (a) The person offering help has already found a place in the group and may be on his or her way to finding a place in the larger world; and (b) the help offered reflects an increase in social interest and self-esteem.

REFERENCES

Adler, A. (1923). Die tragfahigkeit der menschlichen seele [Degree of tolerance of the human soul]. *International Journal of Individual Psychology, 2*(2), 42.

Adler, A. (1927). *The practice and theory of individual psychology.* New York: Harcourt, Brace.

Adler, A. (1930). *The science of living.* London: George Allen & Unwin.

Adler, A. (1938). *Social interest: The challenge to mankind.* London: Faber & Faber.

Adler, A. (1957). *Understanding human nature* (W. B. Wolfe, Trans.). New York: Premier Books. (Original work published 1927)

Adler, A. (1959). *What life should mean to you.* New York: Capricorn. (Original work published 1931)

Adler, A. (1970). The case of Mrs. A. In H. L. Ansbacher & R. R. Ansbacher (Eds.), *Superiority and social interest* (rev. ed., pp. 160–170). Evanston, IL: Northwestern University Press.

Adler, A. (1996). What is neurosis? *Individual Psychology, 54*(4), 318–333. (Original work published 1935)

American Counseling Association. (1995). *Code of ethics and standards of practice*. Alexandria, VA: Author.

Ansbacher, H. L. (1992). Alfred Adler's concepts of community feeling and social interest and the relevance of community feeling for old age. *Individual Psychology, 48*(4), 402–412.

Ansbacher, H. L., & Ansbacher, R. R. (Eds.). (1956). *The individual psychology of Alfred Adler*. New York: Basic Books.

Association for Specialists in Group Work. (1989). *Ethical guidelines for group counselors*. Alexandria, VA: Author.

Bitter, J. R., Christensen, O. C., Hawes, C., & Nicoll, W. G. (1998). Adlerian brief therapy with individuals, couples, and families. *Directions in Clinical and Counseling Psychology, 8*(8), 95–112.

Bitter, J. R., & Nicoll, W. G. (2000). Adlerian brief therapy with individuals: Process and Practice. *Journal of Individual Psychology, 56*(1), 31–44.

Bitter, J. R., Roberts, A., & Sonstegard, M. A. (2002). Adlerian family therapy. In J. Carlson, & D. Kjos (Eds.), *Theories and strategies of family therapy* (pp. 41–70). Boston: Allyn & Bacon.

Bitter, J. R., & West, J. D. (1979). An interview with Heinz Ansbacher. *Journal of Individual Psychology, 35*(1), 95–110.

Clark, A. J. (2002). *Early recollections: Theory and practice in counseling and psychotherapy*. New York: Brunner-Routledge.

Corsini, R. J. (1955). Historic background of group psychotherapy. *Group Psychotherapy, 8*, 219–255.

Corsini, R. J. (1966). *Role playing in psychotherapy*. Chicago: Aldine.

Dinkmeyer, D. C., Jr., & Carlson, J. (2001). *Consultation: Creating school-based interventions*. Philadelphia: Brunner-Routledge.

Dreikurs, R. (1946). *The challenge of marriage*. New York: Hawthorn.

Dreikurs, R. (1959). Early experiments with group psychotherapy: A historical review. *American Journal of Group Psychotherapy, 13*(4), 882–891.

Dreikurs, R. (1960). *Group psychotherapy and group approaches: Collected papers*. Chicago: Alfred Adler Institute.

Dreikurs, R. (1961). The Adlerian approach to therapy. In M. I. Stein (Ed.), *Contemporary psychotherapies* (pp. 80–94). Glencoe, IL: Free Press.

Dreikurs, R. (1971). *Social equality: The challenge of today*. Chicago: Henry Regnery.

Dreikurs, R. (1997). Holistic medicine. *Individual Psychology, 53*(2), 127–205.

Dreikurs, R., & Mosak, H. H. (1967). The tasks of life II: The fourth life task. *Individual Psychologist, 4*, 18–22.

Eckstein, D., & Baruth, L. (1996). *The theory and practice of lifestyle assessment*. Dubuque, IA: Kendall/Hunt.

Grunwald, B., & McAbee, H. (1985). *Guiding the family: Practical counseling techniques*. Muncie, IN: Accelerated Development.

Hoffman, E. (1994). *The drive for self: Alfred Adler and the founding of Individual Psychology*. Reading, MA: Addison Wesley.

McGoldrick, M., Watson, M., & Benton, W. (1999). Siblings through the life cycle. In B. Carter & M. McGoldrick (Eds.), *The expanded family life cycle: Individual, family, and social perspectives* (3rd ed., pp. 153–168). Boston: Allyn & Bacon.

Mosak, H. (1958). Early recollections as a projective technique. *Journal of Projective Techniques, 22*, 302–311.

Mosak, H. H., & Dreikurs, R. (1967). The life tasks III: The fifth life task. *Individual Psychologist, 5*, 16–22.

Pelonis, P. (2002). *Facing change in the journey of life*. Athens, Greece: Fytraki Publications.

Phillips, A. S., & Phillips, C. R. (2000). Birth order differences in self-attributions for achievement. *Journal of Individual Psychology, 56*(4), 474–480.

Polster, M. (1999). Gestalt therapy: Evolution and application. In E. Polster & M. Polster (Eds.), *From the radical center: The heart of Gestalt therapy: Selected writings of Erving and Miriam Polster* (pp. 96–115). Cleveland, OH: Gestalt Institute of Cleveland Press.

Powers, R. L., & Griffith, J. (1987). *Understanding lifestyle: The psycho-clarity process*. Chicago: AIAS.

Powers, R. L., & Griffith, J. (1995). *IPCW: The individual psychology client workbook (with supplements)*. Chicago: AIAS. (Original work published 1986)

Satir, V. (1983). *Conjoint family therapy* (3rd ed.). Palo Alto, CA: Science and Behavior Books.

Selye, H. (1974). *Stress without distress*. New York: Signet.

Shifron, R. (2003, July). *Managing life changes*. Presentation at the Adlerian Summer School, Clonmel, Ireland.

Shulman, B. H., & Mosak, H. H. (1988). *A manual for lifestyle assessment*. Muncie, IN: Accelerated Development.

Sonstegard, M. A., Bitter, J. R., Pelonis-Peneros, P. P., & Nicoll, W. G. (2001). Adlerian group psychotherapy: A brief therapy approach. *Directions in Clinical and Counseling Psychology, 11*(2), 11–24.

Sweeney, T. J. (1998). *Adlerian counseling: A practitioner's approach* (4th ed.). Philadelphia: Accelerated Development.

Terner, J., & Pew, W. L. (1978). *The courage to be imperfect: The life and work of Rudolf Dreikurs*. New York: Hawthorn.

White, M. (Speaker). (2000). *Schizophrenia/severely disturbed patients* (Cassette Recording No. EP00-TP17). Phoenix, AZ: Milton H. Erickson Foundation.

Yalom, I. D. (1995). *The theory and practice of group psychotherapy* (4th ed.). New York: Basic Books.

NOTE

1. Regardless of where twins come in a family, we are interested in how each person perceives the experience of being a twin. If they know who came out first and by how many minutes or seconds, we generally expect that they have separated into a sequential place within the family constellation. For example, if the twins are firstborns, one will be the oldest and one will be the second.

CHAPTER 4

The Practice of Adlerian Group Counseling and Therapy[1]

In this chapter, we:

- Review the history of groups in general and Adlerian group counseling and therapy specifically.
- Define the difference we apply to the terms *group counseling* and *group therapy*.
- Consider Adlerian theory as it directly relates to the practice of Adlerian group counseling and therapy.
- Address the logistics of group practice.
- Note the essential traits and abilities required for effective group leadership in the Adlerian model, including:
  - Presence.
  - Assertiveness and confidence.
  - Courage and risk.
  - Acceptance, interest, and caring.
  - Modeling and collaboration.
  - Adaptability and a sense of humor.
  - Listening teleologically.
  - Working in holistic patterns.
  - Tending the group process.
- Look at Adler's conceptualizations of community feeling and social interest as a basis for the ethical practice of group leaders.

The group approach proposed here is part of a theoretical orientation that has been called Adlerian counseling, Adlerian psychology, Individual Psychology, and the teleoanalytic approach (Manaster & Corsini, 1982; Sweeney, 1998). Regardless of name, the approach extends from the original work of Alfred Adler (1931, 1927/1957) and Rudolf Dreikurs (1950/1953, 1960). As we noted earlier, Adler originated large-group process and reorientation work in his child guidance clinics in Vienna (Terner & Pew, 1978). This large, open-forum, group model became the basis for family education centers developed by Dreikurs and his associates in the United States and Canada (Christensen, 1993; Dreikurs, Corsini, Lowe, & Sonstegard, 1959). Adler's psychology was *holistic*; his model required counselors and therapists to understand the human organism as a whole: a complete person living in a given context, at a specific time in history, within a distinct culture, and perceiving the world from the vantage points provided by heredity, birth order, and gender. In this sense, he was the first systemic therapist. To understand any individual necessitates knowing the person within the entire field in which he or she operates.

Adler also incorporated Vaihinger's (1924/1968) notion of "fictions" into his theory of psychological motivation (Adler, 1920/1959). Rejecting Freud's theory of drives (or instincts[2]), Adler posited a human being who creates goals, both immediate and long-term, that motivate both behavior and development. These goals—especially the long-term ones—guided a person's movement toward an envisioned completion (or self-actualization) and sometimes even toward perfection. Because people rarely reach either completion or perfection, the goals were always fictions, pictures of personal fulfillment adopted "as if" they were absolute and true.

Adler's belief in human teleology was a radical departure from the "cause-and-effect" determinism of science at the beginning of the 20th century. By the middle of the century, however, goal orientation had been confirmed in many areas. Bronowski (1973) highlighted the phenomenal development over millions of years of the frontal lobes, that part of the human brain used for problem solving, planning, and anticipating outcomes (also see Ratay, 2001).

Because individual goal formation starts relatively early in life (Adler thought by the age of 5 or 6 [Ansbacher & Ansbacher, 1956]), relatively few people and situations influence the development of each person's goals and movement. Parents and family members (Gottman, 1997), socioeconomic status (Hart & Risley, 1995), peers and educational experience seem to have the greatest impact. All of these, however, are subject to the creative interpretations of each individual. At the end of the 20th century, Adler's socio-teleological approach with its emphasis on personal hermeneutics provides a perfect foundation for group work.

Group counseling and therapy in the strictest sense is a comparatively recent development. Gazda (1989) traced its origins to the early guidance movement started by Parsons around 1908, and noted that group dynamics really had its heyday in the 1970s. Group methods were not unknown, however, in remote ages. The Greek philosophers referred to the positive effects of group experiences in their writings (Copleston, 1959). There is some evidence that group approaches were used by Ethiopian priests. Even the Marquis de Sade wrote and directed plays that were performed by his fellow inmates at the Chorenton Mental Asylum with therapeutic results noted (Corsini, 1957). Indeed, any time a political or social democracy emerges, group procedures begin to take form. Group counseling "is both the child and the midwife of democracy, requiring a society based on freedom and equality in order to flourish while at the same time perpetuating those ideals" (Sonstegard, Dreikurs, & Bitter, 1982, p. 508).

By way of definition. Within the teleoanalytic orientation, the processes of group therapy and group counseling are very similar, particularly if adolescents and adults comprise the members. Where a distinction is required, therapy is more complete and is directed at changing the faulty lifestyles or personalities of the members. These groups are more common in hospitals and community agencies or clinics where more discouraged and often disturbing clients are seen. Group counseling, on the other hand, does not endeavor to bring about changes in personality; rather, the focus is on the immediate situation, emphasizing self-concept and the discovery of personal motivation. Given this definition, group counseling is the treatment of choice for most adolescents and adults. It is the only useful group process with children whose goals are almost always immediate (Dreikurs, 1950/1953, 1948/1958), and therefore more easily discovered and modified or redirected. Motivation modification follows from the recognition that humans make mistakes, and that mistaken notions and intentions sometimes need correcting. Because we are born in and live most of our lives in groups, this modality holds the most promise for reorientation.

When motivation is modified, behavior change occurs naturally. Indeed, a focus on the patterns and goals of the various group members often leads to changes in a whole range of behaviors. The unity of the personality guarantees that changes in motivation and behavior will be both internally consistent and contiguous (Adler, 1926/1972). Any given behavior, therefore, is understood to be one manifestation of a complete life in movement. When human life is viewed holistically, an individual's behavior never becomes more important than the person.

THE THEORY BEHIND ADLERIAN GROUP PRACTICE

We already noted that Adlerians maintain a socio-teleological perspective: Humans are social beings for whom every communication, behavior, and feeling has a purpose. Adler (1920/1959) used the term *Individual Psychology* to emphasize this holism. It was meant to denote the indivisibility of the person. Similar to the thinking of Polster (1995), Adlerians recognize that individuals have thinking processes, feelings and emotions, behavioral patterns, traits and characteristics, developing and fundamental selves, and definitive mental functions. Still, there is a person who is more than the sum of all of these, a unique being who interprets, chooses, creates, and moves in the real world, in real social contexts. This person sets personal goals, determines her or his own movement, and expresses self differently in different situations, but consistently with one's past experiences, present attitudes, and anticipations about the future. This socio-teleological perspective implies self-determination.

Neither consciousness nor awareness is required for most physical or psychological operations. Humans tend to function economically; they are consciously aware only of what they want or need to know. Indeed, nonconsciousness often facilitates a fluidity of movement. Because all abilities and faculties are in the service of personal intentions, the mind and body function together (Dreikurs, 1997); the ability to think and to feel is available without the requirement of consciousness.

Adler appears to have had a significant influence on Maslow (Hoffman, 1994). Their conceptualizations of motivational processes have some striking parallels. Maslow's (1954/1987) hierarchy of needs suggests that the child first accounts for physiological necessities and safety. After that, a sense of belonging primarily motivates early behavior. In the process, self-esteem results and the individual is able to meet cognitive and aesthetic needs on the road to self-actualization.

Adler and Dreikurs differ slightly in emphasis on what motivates early childhood development. In the struggle to survive and meet basic physiological and safety needs, the child incurs inferiority feeling and seeks to compensate, to overcome, to strive for a better position: This is Adler's position (Ansbacher & Ansbacher, 1964/1979). Dreikurs (1950/1953) placed a stronger emphasis on the need of the child to belong, especially within the family. In either case, human qualities develop as expressions of social living, as movement toward or away from others.

As people get older, the self-created, fictional, final goal of completion (self-actualization or perfection) unifies the personality and supersedes both compensation (striving for superiority) and the need to belong as the primary personal motivation. The value of one's life goal and pattern is determined by the degree to which it is infused with "community feeling" (Ansbacher, 1992) and the action line of community feeling, *social interest*. This feeling permits and stimulates a full social interaction.

Adler thought this feeling to be innate (Ansbacher & Ansbacher, 1956, 1964/1979). It was restricted only by self-absorption, exaggerated feelings of inferiority or superiority in relation to others, and fear of failure, all of which created doubt about one's place within the group. Instead of being free to participate in social groups, restricted individuals feel forced to defend themselves against a wide range of social demands. Maladjustment and dysfunction result from feeling discouraged in relation to others. Indeed, symptomatic behavior is often a safeguard against a loss of prestige, anticipated failure, or an open admission of antisocial or asocial intentions (Adler, 1996a, 1996b).

Self-deception about one's intentions is a normal human process. Awareness of our motives almost always leads to change. A nonconscious subjectivity supports incorporated life patterns and allows us to easily participate in social living. We need a biased apperception to move with conviction toward any goal. We are hermeneutic beings: Our whole personality is based on our subjective interpretations of life. Each individual's basic concept of self in relation to the world, one's personal orientation toward social living, is expressed in a discernible pattern. It is this pattern that Adler (1920/1959, 1927/1957, 1931) called the *lifestyle*. Fundamental notions, convictions, and assumptions underlie the lifestyle pattern and form the *private logic* on which the person operates. The Adlerian counselor works with both the pattern and the logic that supports it in an effort to facilitate a more socially useful life.

ADLERIAN GROUPS: PROCESS AND PRACTICE

Group counseling differs in process depending on the orientation and theoretical formulations of the counselor. Many different processes have proven to be useful (Corey, 2000, 2001; Corey & Corey, 2002; Yalom, 1995). Adlerian groups are characterized by a deliberate attempt to reorient faulty living patterns and instill a better understanding of the principles that stimulate useful interactions and cooperation. This is most commonly implemented through a modification of mistaken motivations as well as the mistaken notions that each person develops and maintains. This constitutes *reorientation*, a change in a group member's attitude toward a present life situation and the problems that must be faced. In this sense, reorientation is an educational experience, a *reeducation* or *relearning*.

In Adlerian group work, learning follows from action; group participation is the necessary action for therapeutic effects. Participation may be either verbal or nonverbal in nature. What a member says is not nearly as important as the attention, presence, and awareness that the person brings to the group process. By attending to other members, the group leader, and the process, even nonverbal participants may take some clarification of a problem away from the group. Further, Adlerian group leaders tend to be quite active in initial group sessions, conducting psychological investigations, offering psychological disclosures, guiding group assessment and "feedback." These interventions can provide new insights—even for those who only listen. Although participation in the broadest sense of the term, therefore, is required, verbal expression is never demanded of or forced from a group member.

Group techniques are more imperative in a democratic society where the authority of the individual is replaced by the authority of the group (Sonstegard, 1998a). Even though we have had a political democracy for centuries, we have a long way to go in implementing a social democracy. The class system is still alive and functioning in the United States (Hart & Risley, 1995). We live in a society still struggling with the remnants of an aristocratic history: A high premium is placed on prestige. The group experience minimizes the requirement for and significance of self-elevation. The group experience attempts to eliminate vanity and the anxiety that people have about status. It helps to free a group member from the vertical movement in which she or he constantly measures self against others. Group process is about generating the respectful, cooperative, and useful social values required for democratic living.

Group counseling and therapy must have structure (see chap. 3). Because group process depends on member involvement and interaction, structure acts more as a guide for the counselor/therapist than mandated stages. Modeling and a liberal use of open questions are the single most important procedures for guiding and implementing structure. Adlerian group counselors seek to (a) establish and maintain a group relationship; (b) examine the patterns and purposes of group members' actions or behaviors; (c) disclose to individuals the goals pursued, and the private logic that supports them; and (d) implement a reorientation that may increase one's community feeling and social interest.

Relationship

Neither democracy nor social equality rests on the assumption of "sameness" (Dreikurs, 1961/1971). Each person in the group will be different from the others, and the leader will be different from the participants, hopefully in especially significant ways related to leadership. What democracy and social equality do require are mutual respect and involvement. Effective groups are not characterized by members who do whatever they please: This is only chaos and sometimes anarchy. Groups, like democratic countries, rely on skilled, firm, but kind leadership. The best leadership happens when those people with more experience and a sense of democratic process guide those with less experience, a leadership most often accomplished through modeling.

Relationship is more than the establishment of contact and rapport, although these are very important functions. Group counselors must create an opportunity for *voice* (Gilligan, 1982) without imposing the requirement of voice; groups will naturally develop an atmosphere for *connected knowing* (Goldberger, Tarule, Clinchy, & Belenky, 1996) when the group leader attends to the development of each person's voice. This process also supports the development of common tasks to which the group leader must win the cooperation of the participants. Group process facilitates cooperation and collaboration. Maintaining it requires constant vigilance.

Social connectedness is the common result of group counseling and therapy. As a member listens to someone else discuss a personal problem, a new understanding or awareness may be fostered in the listener. This is a phenomenon uniquely associated with group process. The one-to-one relationships of individual therapy often preclude listening without defensiveness. Similarly, when marital and family therapy sessions involve single units, each member tends to listen with the intent of maintaining a desired position in the relationship or system. Indeed, only those family models that employ group process (e.g., a reflecting team [Andersen, 1991] or Adlerian family counseling in an open forum [Christensen, 1993]) are able to create a therapeutic "pause" in which real listening can occur. A bonding in shared experiences—or even shared difficulties—follows from identifying with others, understanding feelings, and accepting a diversity of ideas. In turn, this bonding leads to more participation and to universalization, the cementing element responsible for group cohesiveness.

Psychological Assessment

Adlerian group counselors use any number of different assessment techniques, most of which were developed as an implementation of Individual Psychology. We use the concept of assessment here, because it implies an understanding of the whole as opposed to an analysis of parts. Indeed, with a socio-teleological perspective, any part of the assessment should produce clues to each person's goals, purposes, and lifestyle. Adlerians have always relied on assessments of family constellation, birth order, early recollections, relational difficulties, dreams, and artwork to understand individual movement. More recent discoveries include a differential diagnosis based on "The Question" (see Dreikurs, 1997, pp. 165–168), an evaluation of body movement and personality priorities (Kfir, 1981; Schoenaker & Schoenaker, 1975), and remembered fairy tales or folk stories. Each of these lines of inquiry can reveal a group member's interpretations of self, life, and the world, as well as any mistaken notions that may be connected to these interpretations.

The following group process illustrates the meaning that can emerge during a teleological assessment process. In a counseling group, Lynn commented that she thought she could "be more effective and be getting more out of life." As group members asked her why she felt this way, she related some recurring dreams she had been having; in each one, she was little, and whether she was standing in front of her teacher, mother, or father, none of them were ever happy with her—no matter what she did.

The counselor asked if Lynn could remember anything that happened when she was a little girl. Lynn offered several early recollection, one of which reported a time, at age 5, when she was asked to sing for her mother's friends; she opened her mouth, but nothing would come out. The counselor asked the group members what her memories might mean. When no possibilities were forthcoming, the counselor suggested that "perhaps Lynn was restricted in her activity to only those things she already knew would please others and would be certain to reflect favorably on her." Lynn listened carefully, but did not comment. Others disagreed with the counselor, saying that Lynn was much too independent, too poised and sure of herself. She was considered a leader, and she was "positively dynamic" in her pursuit of activities.

In a later session, however, Lynn talked about what the disclosure had meant to her: "I think it may be true. I do feel inclined to do only those things that please. I'm kind of concerned about my image, how I project myself. I would like to be less concerned about image, to do what is right regardless of how others feel."

Group counseling or psychotherapy with adolescents and adults can easily proceed from discussions initiated by group members. In the normal course of conversation, the leader will find many opportunities to develop a line of inquiry that can lead to psychological understanding. Children, on the other hand, often need a tighter focus.

Adlerians typically provide this focus in children's groups with an inquiry about mistaken goals (Dreikurs, 1940, 1941). Dreikurs' four goals (attention getting, power struggle, revenge, and assumed disability) and their recognition have been delineated elsewhere (Dreikurs, 1948/1958; Dreikurs & Soltz, 1964). These goals account for most of childhood misbehavior, because they do not require conscious implementation. I (Jim) have suggested some conscious motivations of children, an enhancement of Dreikurs' four goals: the conscious motivations are *self-elevation*, *getting*, and *avoidance* (Bitter, 1991).

Although the counseling of children has typically occurred in family sessions, group sessions often provide a unique glimpse of the child's pattern with peers. In contrast to the limited interaction the counselor experiences when talking directly to a child, individually or in a family, the group provides an arena that showcases the child in action. Children may be able to act "properly" around adults, but much of the veneer the child uses to cover up is stripped away in a group setting.

We give a more detailed account of group practice with children in the next chapter. Here, we only wish to provide an example that demonstrates the advantage of a group setting with children: It illustrates the discovery of a child's conscious goal of self-elevation (see chap. 5).

Jane was bright, and she could be charming. Most of her teachers felt she was a good student; she was assertive, but she never caused trouble. Gerald was in the same elementary classroom as Jane. He, too, was a bright person, but he was also known as one of the "disturbing elements" in the class. Both Jane and Gerald were in the same counseling group.

At the beginning of one group session, the counselor asked the group if another counselor could sit in on the group for one day. The group agreed, and Jane immediately invited the new counselor to sit next to her. Jane took the initiative and subtly began to belittle Gerald while she put herself in a favorable light. This disturbed Gerald, and he began to act up. The other boys took his lead and joined in. Jane had achieved her goal of self-elevation; she sat back with an expression that said, "See how bad they are, and how good I am."

The counselor intervened in the boys' disruption by asking, "I wonder how many of you know what just happened in here?" The counselor and the cocounselor led a discussion that both disclosed Jane's purpose and indicated to the boys how easily they seemed to be drawn into the "bad kid" trap.

Jane's technique, purpose, and pattern would never have been discovered in an individual or family counseling session. She would have been able to present herself in a positive light that would have gone unchallenged. Because no one was really complaining about Jane, it was only in the group setting that her process could be revealed.

Awareness and Psychological Disclosure

Human beings live in groups. They behave in social settings. It is in these settings that the patterns of one's life have meaning. In private, a person can maintain any set of beliefs or convictions, no matter how at odds they are with the general perceptions of others. In private, what one *says* or believes and what one *does* may have no relation whatsoever. In groups, however, members pay more attention to what a person does, and incongruencies in declaration and behavior will be challenged. Adlerian counselors believe that any real change must

The Practice of Adlerian Group Counseling and Therapy

start with awareness. Awareness—of which insight is only one form—is elevating that which is out of awareness, nonconscious, or unconscious (we use these terms interchangeably and as adjectives) to a new level of clarity, focus, and understanding (Polster, 1995; Polster & Polster, 1973). Such awareness is generally not enough in and of itself to foster change, but it is a necessary start.

Awareness is facilitated in groups at several levels. Counselors or therapists may suggest motivations and patterns through psychological disclosures (Dreikurs, 1967). The psychological disclosures discussed with one member may have meaning to others who are "just listening." Group members may offer feedback. A group assessment of interactions right in the group may also lead to new understandings.

In individual therapy, awareness and insight often depend on the relationship with and skill of the therapist. In groups, awareness is regularly achieved through peer response and support. The statements and opinions of group members can easily carry more weight than anything the counselor might say. There is less resistance when feedback comes from peers—especially in adolescent and adult groups. A group consensus carries a powerful impact in respectful confrontation as well as encouragement for change. Further, even difficult awarenesses, when they are shared by others, can be received with less of a burden: A sense of commonality normalizes the meaning of experience.

A 10th grader recognized herself in the discussion with another group member. When asked for feedback, she said, "I am like Jennifer too. I am always helping the teacher, anticipating the right thing to do, and being good. I do this at home, in school, even when I am just hanging out, not because I want to, but because I want to get in good. I worry all the time about people thinking bad things about me." This response from a group member serves both people well. It tells the first member around whom the original discussion occurred that she is not alone, that someone else feels the same way. It also leads to bonding, and an alternative "expert" resource in the pursuit of change.

Regardless of the origin of psychological understanding, the reactions of group members make *the* significant difference in whether awareness, insight, and redirection are achieved. Nothing a counselor might offer is likely to stick if group members find no validity in it. Group members accept interventions from each other, because they feel that a certain equality exists among them. Counselor interventions only gain corrective influence when the active support of the group has been won.

In a Parent "C" group, a father indicated that neither he nor his wife could get their son, Ben, to come home after school to change clothes before going out to play. The child had been spanked, had privileges removed, and nothing had worked. In exasperation, the father had told Ben that the next time he went to play with his friends without first coming to change, "I am going to take your model airplanes down and trample them."

Another parent almost shouted: "You can't do that! That's just mean."

Still another parent suggested that there might be a good reason for Ben's behavior: "I know my son would not like to be left out of his friends' activities just because of this rule about changing clothes."

The counselor inquired: "What do you think of that?"

The father: "I hadn't thought of it that way before, but it makes some sense. Ben has been having some trouble making friends."

Another group member: "You can't control your son at this age—maybe not any age. Why don't you discuss the problem with your son."

Still another: "What's more important to you? A son with friends or a son with clean clothes?" (For more information on Parent "C" Groups, see Dinkmeyer & Carlson, 2001.)

There are a number of ways in which the group leader gains influence in the group, most of which will be discussed later. Psychological disclosure is an area of special concern. If handled badly, counselor initiated psychological disclosure can interrupt or derail group process and can engender group resistance.

A psychological disclosure does not even have to be wrong to be ineffective: Premature disclosures fail because the foundation for receiving them has not been laid. Dreikurs and other well-known Adlerians became so skilled *in demonstrations* at quick assessments and pinpoint disclosures that it was easy to assume that faster was better.

In most cases, however, a group counselor or therapist is far better off asking group members to think about and discuss possible motivations and patterns in each other. It is not uncommon for a group member to provide some real insight; then, the counselor need only affirm it: "I was watching you as people offered ideas, and it seems to me that Amy's point really hit home with you."

Counselor disclosures are required when contributions from group members fail to make essential meaning. In the early sessions of a group, the ideas and comments of group members are often projections of what is happening with or motivating the speaker: These contributions are worth noting for their projective value, but may not prove to be helpful to the member-in-focus.

While it is important for Adlerian group leaders to start forming teleological hypotheses about the group members as soon as possible, experience suggests that it is wise to collect many examples, to look for repeated patterns, and to even see the pattern enacted in the group before offering a disclosure. Even then, Adlerians have long enacted the disclosure/confrontation process *tentatively*, seeking to maintain mutual respect from the leader position, a position the group initially views to have more authority or power. After listening to everyone's ideas, a counselor might use some version of Dreikurs' (1967) disclosure process:

> "I have an idea that is somewhat different from what has been offered. Would you like to hear it?"
>
> Disclosure options start with:
>
> "Perhaps …"
> "Could it be …"
> "I get the impressions that …"

The beauty of this process is that it leaves group members free to consider without feeling that an expert has given the final word. If it fits, the group often responds with statements that affirm and indicate a new understanding. When it does not fit, the group almost always searches for a more accurate interpretation. In either case, the group has been oriented toward a psychological understanding as opposed to merely a social one.

Counselors who engage in psychological disclosure are always taking a *necessary* risk. Credibility with a group does go up and down depending on the accuracy and acceptance of the interpretations. Timing and balance are also important attributes for leaders to develop. Too many counselor disclosures in a session will lessen impact. Offering none in a discussion of a difficult issue can foster confusion and chaos. The leader's risk of being wrong, or using inaccurate language, goes down when she or he has gathered sufficient examples as data, when other group members have offered their opinions, or when interaction in the group has already confirmed the leader's hypothesis. And still, disclosure is a risk.

Reorientation

Reorientation and reeducation are the endpoints of Adlerian counseling and psychotherapy. Adlerian group counseling with children is designed to redirect the mistaken goals of members. Adlerian group counseling and therapy with adolescents and adults seeks to aid members in giving up erroneous concepts about self, life, and dealing with others. Parents and teachers are helped to understand their motivations with children and to find more effective methods for influencing the immature. Indeed, when parents and teachers change their approach, children's relationships with siblings, peers, and adults in general improve. The group is able to cultivate these changes because of the focus on motivation modification as opposed to behavior change.

In the actions and interactions of group members, goals and intentions are expressed; personal social orientations are demonstrated. Adlerians tend to stay with this interactional, systemic focus. Looking for an intrapsychic and unconscious psychological process in children and many adults is not necessary and is usually detrimental. Real problems exist in the social fields in which individuals operate. Purpose is more often revealed in the consequences of action than in introspection.

Many people—especially adolescents—feel alone. Adolescents who experience social isolation also tend to develop negative self-concepts that no amount of adult effort can eliminate. Group process stands in opposition to this situation. Through participation, it seeks to increase one's receptiveness to different ideas; to new facts, concepts, or experiences; to an acceptance of value previously foreign to one's thinking.

> "Since this is the last day of our group this school year, I thought I would tell you about a conversation I had with

my mother. I told her that I didn't think I was stupid anymore. When she asked why I said that, I told her that all of you seemed to think I was smart. Before I joined this group, I thought I was dumb. My mother didn't think that, but they have to like you. None of you actually have to listen to me, but you do, and you seem to mean it."

The nature of personal deficiencies and perceived failures makes *encouragement* the essential factor in all corrective endeavors (see Dinkmeyer & Dreikurs, 1963). When people feel inferior, they lose a sense of place in the community. A competitive culture augments the danger of not measuring up to what society demands; this is especially noticeable in schools where parents, teachers, and even peers increasingly pressure young people to achieve at higher levels. A profoundly discouraged individual requires reassurance in almost every counseling session. This may be accomplished deliberately or as a by-product of the session itself. The success of the group counselor depends to a large extent on his or her ability to provide encouragement. A perfect session, to us, would be one that worked continuously from an encouraging orientation.

Reorientation and reeducation requires a restoration of faith in the members of the group: faith in themselves and each other, a realization of personal strengths and abilities, a sense of dignity and worth. Change is facilitated by the emergence of hope: by seeing that there are options; that different approaches have worked for others; and that life can work out well (optimism). Faith and hope contradict the negative social influences to which people are exposed every day.

Peer encouragement often plays the most significant role in reorientation. Group members impact each other in a myriad of ways: by "being straight" with each other, by creating options and generating new solutions, by acknowledging and appreciating strengths in others, by celebrating accomplishments. Participating in a group almost automatically evokes mutual help. The group is also a place in which individuals can try out new behaviors and new approaches. Through role playing or direct experience, members are able to test themselves.

Perhaps the greatest encouragement comes from feeling that one has found a place in the group: that in spite of differences, each person can be accepted. Under the guidance of the group leader, members learn to cope, to confront and address difficulties and disagreements, to resolve issues. In most instances, this new sense of belonging translates into positive interactions in other parts of life (e.g., the home, work, or the school).

Reorientation and encouragement increase the self-confidence of group members, permitting them to act more decisively, deliberately, and candidly. Confidence that extends from encouragement is never a conceit. It is not a compensation for perceived inferiority. It follows from the conviction that one is worthwhile and cannot be replaced, that others need us, "that you are acting well, and that you are a fellow (hu)man and a true friend" (Ansbacher & Ansbacher, 1978, p. 125).

THE LOGISTICS OF GROUP PROCESS

In this section, we take up the nitty-gritty of Adlerian group counseling and therapy: those areas less defined by theory and research that must be addressed when forming a group and getting it started. These areas include selection of group members, group composition, group size, group setting, length and frequency of sessions. In most of these areas, research is either nonexistent or inconclusive with regard to effectiveness. Nor does Adlerian theory or accepted practice define these parameters. The best we can offer is a glimpse of the process we use when addressing each of these areas.

Selection of Group Members

Groups may be formed in any number of ways. Selection processes will differ from setting to setting based on the needs of the various situations. Some groups are composed of members who feel they have little choice in whether to participate (e.g., court referrals of either first-time offenders or those on probation). Winning cooperation is typically more difficult in these circumstances, because resistance is high. The counselor must be patient and take the attitude that everyone has to be there, so they might as well get something out of it. Some groups are formed to meet specific needs: Community agency groups to help people with depression, eating disorders, or psychosomatic problems, and groups in schools to help children with underachievement are all examples. These groups build cohesiveness based on a shared difficulty, and the leader will have to invest some energy in helping the members use that commonality as a starting point and not a final destination. Some groups may be formed to help essentially functional individuals achieve better relationships through group education; examples of such educational groups include parent study, parent "C," *STEP,* and *Active Parenting* groups; open-forum family education groups; and personal growth groups and marriage enrichment groups. These groups tend to have standardized formats, and membership really depends on a good fit between the goals of the program and the goals of those who attend.

Schools are still one of the primary places in which group counseling occurs. Because groups tend to be more visible in a school setting than individual sessions are, counselors often encounter more resistance from fellow colleagues. Teachers may resent students leaving class to participate in a group program, feeling that something is happening in the group that is beyond their control; secrecy can actually fuel this response. Or they may refer students to group counseling and decide the process is useless if they don't see immediate results. When principals and other administrators refer students, it is not uncommon for the group to consist only of those children who have become significant disturbances in the system.

In general, schools need to be won over to the value of group counseling. This process requires the counselor to become a known and useful entity within the school. A counselor who starts with individual sessions, while also developing effective consultation experiences with teachers and parents, will have less difficulty in winning support for a group counseling program. From individual sessions, it is possible to ask schoolchildren if they would be willing to try a group experience. A small group can be enlarged by asking the youngsters to invite a friend or a classmate; such invitations also provide a measure of safety for the members in the initial sessions.

In general, heterogeneous groups tend to work better in most settings. Life is filled with diversity, and meeting that same diversity in groups makes the experience more real, and hence more useful. A homogeneous group may be composed of "all the people who have a given problem or who have caused problems." The latter groups almost always start with the standard tapes people use to justify their behavior and blame everyone else. The counselor is then the only person who can ultimately challenge their mistaken notions. These same people in a more heterogeneous group will hear different perspectives from the community or their peers, and the counselor will be able to demonstrate a willingness to incorporate this diversity without prejudice.

One of the first questions adolescents often ask is, "Why are we having a group?" Our answer: "We have found that when people have a chance to talk things over in groups, it usually helps."

"Why were we selected?"

"We would like everyone to have a place to talk things over, but there are not enough counselors; so we invite those we feel can profit most from the group meetings."

Wattenburg (1953) was one of the first in the profession of counseling to ask the question "Who needs counseling?" and who will benefit from it. Almost 25 years later, Ohlsen (1977) suggested that this same question was germane to the process of forming a group. Today, pregroup screening and "preparation for group" meetings are close to required, encoded even in our professional standards (see Corey, 2001; Corey & Corey, 2002; Corey, Corey, & Callanan, 2003; Yalom, 1995). Prescreening rests on the notion that only those individuals who will be successfully helped should participate in group counseling or therapy. Although the intake procedures associated with pregroup meetings may provide excellent preparation for group members, the selection process itself fails to provide an opportunity for those who need it the most. The isolated, noncommunicative, or disruptive can only find real solutions to their problems in a group setting; excluding them from group or devising a group of only homogeneous members does little to change dysfunctional patterns. All of us meet difficult people to varying degrees in everyday life. We cope, or we learn to cope. There is no significant need for group members to be protected from difficult people. Indeed, group settings are far better suited to the discovery of new coping strategies than any other venue we find in everyday life.

When possible, groups work best if (a) no one is compelled to join a group, and (b) no one who wishes to join is turned away. As we noted in the earlier chapters, refusing an individual the opportunity to become a group member is contrary to democratic premises (Sonstegard, 1998b; Sonstegard, Dreikurs, & Bitter, 1982).

Group Composition

Adlerians share the general sentiment of the helping professions that heterogeneous groups are more effective, especially in long-term therapy. Yalom (1995) suggests that homogeneity promotes cohesiveness, but that advantage and positive therapeutic outcomes are not necessarily the same.

> *Homogeneous groups will jell more quickly, become more cohesive, offer more immediate support to group members, are better attended, have less conflict, and provide more rapid relief of symp-*

> *toms.* ... The homogeneous group, in contrast to the heterogeneous group, has a tendency to remain at superficial levels and is a less effective medium for the altering of character structure. (p. 255)

Yalom's demarcation clearly indicates that homogeneity is more appropriate in group counseling than group psychotherapy.[3] Homogeneous groups have been successfully conducted for children with school problems, underachievers, and potential dropouts; for couples and marital relationships; for those on court-referred probationary status or first-time offenders; for substance and alcohol abuse; for grief and loss; for posttraumatic stress; and for mild outpatient clinical disorders. In these groups, homogeneity of concern or issue seems to lessen the stigma that is too often attached to a given problem.

Although Adlerians deny no one access to group counseling, several considerations are worth keeping in mind. Unless the group is designed to be gender specific, it is advisable to have an even number of men and women or boys and girls. Such an arrangement provides support for each gender within the group and allows for the development of equality between the sexes. Groups always mirror in some fashion the larger society in which we live, a society that is still largely sexist. Group counselors, therefore, have a special responsibility to make sure that women—and especially young girls—have an acknowledged and respected voice in the group process.

This same principle applies to a diversity of culture, ethnicity, sexual orientation, creed, and socioeconomic level. Where possible, encouraging a balance in diversity and giving voice to that diversity is useful. When groups lead to mutual understanding, the promise of democracy is advanced. The structures of many communities and the institutions within them are all too often limited to a homogeneous culture, and groups in these communities will reflect that culture.

Too divergent an age range among children and adolescents should be avoided. Although there is no evidence that a specific age range is better than others, personal clinical experience suggests that preschool and elementary school children do best with a maximum spread of 3 years. Adolescents and young adults seem to handle a spread of up to 5 years. Because development in youth is more compressed, children and adolescents who are closer in age have similar life experiences and often find it easier to relate to one another. Adults are often able to relate to people much younger than themselves, but find it hard to project their current experience more than a decade into the future.

Temperament and activity level have not been an issue for us in group composition. Extremely withdrawn children, for example, have been mixed in the same group with relatively aggressive, acting-out, or attention-getting youngsters with some advantages for everyone.

Group Size

There is a general clinical perception that 10 to 12 is the maximum limit for effectiveness, with 8 members being a preferred number. Even at 12 members, Yalom (1995) suggested that there is some loss of effectiveness for ongoing therapy groups. On the other hand, Adlerians have conducted group counseling sessions with more than 30 in them with some indications of effectiveness. The upper limit depends to a great extent on the skills and experience of the counselor, the amount of time available for group sessions, and, to some extent, the nature and purpose of the group.

An ongoing, open group for first-time offenders and their parents was held in a juvenile court in St. Albans, West Virginia, from 1975 to 1977. These sessions were conducted with children and adolescents initially in an inner circle and their parents in a nonparticipating outer circle. Halfway through the sessions, the circles reversed and the counselors ran a group session for parents with the children listening. These groups never had less than 15 people in them, and frequently had in excess of 30. In the 18 months for which records were kept, only one first-time offender was arrested a second time, and both parents and children reported a better understanding of each other.

A lower limit on group size is determined by the need for group functioning. Yalom (1995) suggested that five is the lower limit for effective group process. Below that number, the sessions tend to become individual counseling or therapy with fellow clients watching. We believe that five members are enough for the diversity of interaction and opinion necessary for motivation modification and to provide peer encouragement for change and reorientation.

Educationally focused groups have been successfully applied to sessions in which more than 100 people were in attendance. Such groups include parent and family education groups (Christensen, 1993), *STEP* groups (Dinkmeyer & McKay, 1997), *Active Parenting* groups (Popkin, 1993); psychodramatic groups such as family reconstruction groups (Satir, Bitter, & Krestensen, 1988), and Adlerian social therapy experiences (Schoenaker & Schoenaker, 1975). We also have seen great value in the procedures developed for experiential learning with a large audience (see Satir, 1983). These groups shared certain commonalities: (a) Almost all of the participants were adults; (b) all were functional and shared a common interest in the group process; and (c) all sought to improve their lives with new information and experiences.

Group Setting

Atmosphere in a group counseling or therapy room is worth attending to. It can support and augment group process or distract. Some institutions simply can't supply ideal space, but some minimum requirements are essential. These include (a) privacy; (b) reasonable control of outside noise, inside temperature, and lighting; and (c) the opportunity for participants to sit in a circle. Faced with crowded school and agency conditions, we have held group counseling sessions in storage rooms, outside boiler rooms, on auditorium stages, and in isolated corridors, but these are not the places in which groups function best.

An ideal meeting room is carpeted, for both comfort and sound insulation. The lighting should be sufficient to allow everyone to see easily without glare, and some access to outside light is always a plus. The chairs should be appropriate to the size of the participants, comfortable, but not so comfortable that members are encouraged to drift off. There should be a foot or two between chairs, and a minimum of 4 to 5 feet of space between the circle and the walls of the room. In addition to guaranteeing privacy (usually a locked door), the group setting should be free from distractions, such as noise from intercoms, music, and outside activities, free from heavy hallway and corridor traffic, and away from other group activities (e.g., other group counseling or therapy sessions; gyms and exercise or yoga classes; academic or practical training classes; and band, chorus, or orchestra practice). We also try to avoid sitting around a table, although some of the newer round tables have been adequately designed for group work. Rectangular tables always make it difficult for group members to stay in contact with each other: Someone or some set of people is always lost.

Many modern facilities in universities, community agencies, hospitals, training centers, and even some schools have observation rooms, most with one way mirrors and/or video monitors. These facilities may be used by students and counselors or therapists-in-training, other colleagues, and even reflecting teams. When observers are involved, it is important for the group leader to show the group members every part of the facilities in use, complete with an explanation of how the equipment works and is used. This disclosure includes introducing the group members to the people who will be engaged in either participatory or silent (nonparticipatory) observations. People make up what they suspect but do not know. Fully informed consent not only protects the individual members, but also reduces unnecessary anxiety in the group. In most cases, some kind of release from participants will be required.

There is always at least an initial distraction any time observation processes are employed. Most of this distraction disappears in a very short time. When the number of people observing is small, Yalom (1995) recommended, and we concur, that these people be seated in the group session room. It is important that the group know from the beginning the manner in which the observers will participate and that the observers stick to that arrangement. Also, when observers are in the group room, their attendance must be as regular as that of the group leader.

Frequency, Length, and Duration of Group Sessions

As in so many other logistical areas of group process, the information related to time has produced scattered results. Although many time-extended groups (e.g., "marathons," weekend groups, week-long groups) have been used by Adlerians in the past, the popularity of these groups faded after the early 1970s (Yalom, 1995). Many groups in schools, community agencies, hospitals, and correctional facilities are open groups with a continuously changing membership. These groups require a certain flexibility in the leader and the group members, and acknowledgment of session-to-session changes is important for smooth transitions. Closed groups are usually limited in a couple of ways: The membership is set at the beginning of the group session(s) and does not vary; and a specific number of sessions over a set number of weeks with a clear ending point is established. Closed groups may become a refuge from the demands of outside living, a place members come to count on for replenishment.

It is also not uncommon for time itself to affect closed-group process. In a closed group, setting an exact number of sessions of a specific duration with a clear termination point sets a boundary on the group experience. In the early session(s), presenting difficulties (i.e., problems, symptoms, dysfunctional coping, even disorders) may quickly diminish or disappear altogether. Group members, feeling that they have all the time in the world, will focus on building relationships and finding a place within the group. When the midpoint of the group sessions is reached, symptoms and problems may be reasserted in group as members sense they are running out of time. It is in this latter phase that the real psychological work of the group occurs, and closure is sought and reached before termination.

The most common format for groups is weekly sessions happening over 12 to 14 weeks for somewhere between 1 and 2 hours each. Less than an hour: The group seldom has time to warm up and accomplish anything useful. More than 2 hours: Fatigue sets in—for both the group members and the leader. In academic settings, a semester is often used for the duration of a group. School administrators often try to limit groups to a single class period. This is generally enough for preschool and elementary school, but too short for middle school and high school: In these preadolescent and adolescent years, counselors should win support for groups extending over two class periods.

It is especially critical in schools to adhere to the time schedule. This supports a seriousness of effort in the group process and allows the rest of the school to meet the requirements of the day efficiently, without undue disruption. No group counseling program in a school has survived without the support of teachers and other school administrators. Straying from agreements about time and frequency of meetings is one of the fastest ways to lose outside support.

THE ROLE OF THE GROUP COUNSELOR OR THERAPIST

Counseling and therapy are like few other vocations in that the *personhood* of the therapist is integral to the practice of the profession. To be effective as a group leader, the counselor/therapist must constantly develop *who* he or she is as well as *what* group skills are used. In the Adlerian model, the person and practice cannot be separated. This is not to indicate that only one type of person with a singular approach can be an Adlerian group leader. Indeed, a wide range of people and personalities can be successful. All of these people, however, have a tendency to share certain personal orientations and commitments to the work.

A number of authors have described the values, characteristics, and skills essential to the group counselor (Corey & Corey, 2002; Yalom, 1995) and to counselors and therapists in general (Corey & Corey, 2003; Mozdzierz, Lisiecki, Bitter, & Williams, 1986; Satir, 1983).

In the following paragraphs, we delineate many of these counselor attributes from an Adlerian perspective. Most of these descriptions directly parallel Adler's social imperatives, his *community feeling* and its action line *social interest* (Adler, 1938; Ansbacher, 1992; Ansbacher & Ansbacher, 1964/1979).

Presence

The group counselor must start by bringing all of his or her attention to the people and the process in the group. Satir (1983) talked about using all of her senses to take people in, and this is as significant in group process as it is in family therapy. We find it useful to orient ourselves to the people and tasks at hand:

- Who is sitting in the circle?
- What do their faces say?
- What stance do their bodies take?
- Whose body posture is paired with whom?
- How do people return a greeting?
- With whom do people sit?
- Who's talking to whom?
- Do there appear to be alliances?
- Do some people seem quiet, withdrawn, antagonistic, suspicious, or isolated?

All of these questions orient the leader toward an understanding of individuals and an initial tending of the group process. They orient the counselor outward, away from self-concerns or performance issues, toward psychological contact.

Further, the group leader must genuinely like people, feel comfortable in the company of others, bring an accepting presence to the process, and enjoy mutual give and take (interaction), whether it be congenial or controversial. Where possible and appropriate, it includes the communication of an appreciation for others. This stance allows counselors and therapists to be both firm and kind in their interpersonal relationships. The group leader must "be perceived by the other person(s) as trustworthy, as dependable or consistent in some deep sense" (Rogers, as cited in Kirschenbaum & Henderson, 1989, p. 119).

Assertiveness and Confidence

Although there is no specific personality type that a group counselor or therapist must *be*, it is difficult to visualize a shy or reticent person achieving any measure of success. Group counseling, especially as applied to children and teenagers, requires a certain degree of assertiveness. Assertiveness is different than being directive or controlling. It has to do with bringing an interested and involved presence to the group, talking in a clear and even voice, and communicating interest without defensiveness. It is a willingness to set limits and establish an order in the service of psychological freedom. It is being comfortable with leadership without an insistence on being the leader.

A useful assertiveness flows naturally from an integrated self-confidence, a confidence based on optimism. Group counselors must have faith in the process, in their ability to handle even difficult situations calmly and without fear of being tested, challenged, or defeated by others. The projection of such confidence is especially important when working with children, adolescents, discouraged members, and others who draw on the leader's strength for an initial sense of stability.

Certain internalizations rob counselors of their confidence and effectiveness. Confidence is often a matter of focus; it is easily lost in questions that run counter to a quality presence and psychological contact: "How am I doing?" "What will others think of me?" "Will I do as well as someone else?" "Am I doing group *the right way?*" A counselor can never live up to the standards involved in such self-scrutiny. It makes us the same as all those helpless creatures who get caught in our headlights on a dark road at night: We are immobilized, unable to assess the situation or to make adequate decisions. Although a certain level of self-concern is common when first learning group leadership, even then it is useful to focus on the group by preprogramming very pragmatic internalizations. Ask:

- "With whom am I sharing this experience?"
- "What interests me about them?"
- "What do I need to do first?"

Courage and Risk

Courage is usually the foundation for assertiveness and confidence. Group counselors always need the courage of their convictions. A note of caution must be introduced here, because courage and conviction is not the same as *playing God*, imposing authority, or taking absolute positions. Conviction walks hand-in-hand with respect. Unless counselors have respect for themselves, they cannot expect the same from members of the group. A conviction in the soundness of group process leaves the counselor free to listen, allows the therapist to stay calm and relaxed while he or she observes the dynamics of group interaction and the verbal and nonverbal participation of group members.

The heart of Adlerian psychological interventions involves *guessing*, suggesting possible motivations or patterns that make sense out of the behaviors and experiences of individuals in the group. Adlerian counselors engage in *soft confrontations*, disclosures offered with respect and tentativeness. Still, every intervention, whether a reflection, question, clarification, or interpretation, involves a risk, the possibility of being wrong. The nature of group process requires the leader to intervene more often during initial sessions than in later ones. Again, early guidance and activating a group presence involves risk. And risk requires courage.

For the Adlerian approach to work, the group counselor assumes the responsibility of serving as a model, an interpreter, and a guiding agent in the psychological process of change. It is a role function to direct, when necessary, the group's interaction into meaningful channels and an understanding of what is taking place. If a counselor fails to assume this role, an entire session can be spent in frivolous talk.

The counselor must bring to the process every mastered skill and rely on an educated intuition, sensing when to permit group members to proceed undirected in their explorations and when guidance is required. Asking the right question at the right moment is a skill that generally only comes with experience. In general, those questions that increase group interaction, make the general more specific, transform group discussions into psychological explorations, or reframe options and choices are the ones a leader seeks.

The goal for the Adlerian group counselor is *reasonable risk*. Before disclosing a motive, goal, or pattern, it is useful to have tested the possibility in several indirect ways. Does a motive or goal appear to be guiding the member's behavior in several different places, instances, or situations? Does the pattern of coping or living repeat itself over time? Does understanding a motivation or process help the leader to predict certain behaviors or actions in the group? If the counselor starts to form teleological hypotheses early and tests them regularly throughout the sessions, the accuracy of psychological disclosures is all but assured.

The courage to intervene follows from what Dreikurs (1970) called *the courage to be imperfect*: It is the courage to be wrong and admit error; to experience the disagreement of others; to reconsider and correct faulty impressions, interpretations, or the language of one's interventions. Group counselors can have this courage because of the democratic and egalitarian atmosphere generated in groups. The process of making a difference in members' lives does not depend on one person.

Acceptance, Interest, and Caring

Human beings spend a lot of time in systems and institutions permeated with criticism and authoritarian structures. Families, schools, religions, work settings, and local communities are all too often prime examples of this harshness. Group counseling and therapy must always be the antidote to such negative experiences and situations. Adlerian group counselors seek to replace critical, negative judgments with an empathic understanding. Adler quoted an unidentified English author in describing his model for working with people: "To see with the eyes of another, to hear with the ears of another, to feel with the heart of another" (Ansbacher & Ansbacher, 1964/1979, p. 42). The communication of empathic understanding lays a foundation for a feeling of acceptance in group members. In group, anything can be said, anything expressed, and someone, perhaps many, will be trying to listen and understand.

When group members live in or come from severely punishing environments and experiences, trust in the group as an alternative can be long in coming. We have personally worked slowly and carefully for over a year to build a safe place of acceptance for adolescents who had been placed in a "school of last resort," a placement little more than a large detention center.

Acceptance, in an Adlerian sense, has many of the same properties as, but still differs from, *unconditional positive regard*, which even Rogers acknowledged could only be fully realized in theory (Kirschenbaum & Henderson, 1989). There are many positions a group member will take, or behaviors enacted, that cannot be viewed as positive or useful. In the group session, the person is heard and does not lose a place in the group even when others express disagreement.

Children, adolescents, and discouraged individuals often have a difficult time separating a dislike for their actions from a dislike for them personally. The counselor's focus on understanding motivation makes it possible for these individuals to learn and grow without losing self-esteem or self-respect. Indeed, the counselor's interest expressed in teleological explorations eschews the critical assessments of "good, bad, right, wrong." The experience for the member is that someone cares, is interested in her or his well-being and welfare.

Modeling and Collaboration

All of the characteristics already discussed must be natural and fully integrated parts of the counselor. The sensitivity, caring, interest, acceptance, confidence, and courage must be genuine, and to make a difference, they must be actively modeled. Constructive group process is more often *caught* from the group leader than taught. To the extent that group members feel the positive effects of the leader's interventions, they begin to use them with each other.

Group members also quickly sense whether the process is collaborative or leader centered. How the group starts and is maintained in the first few sessions sets the pattern for most of the rest of the group experience. If the leader's interventions are the only ones that count, group members quickly stop participating. When group members' opinions and contributions are established as meaningful early in the process, the group generates a cohesiveness and openness that is otherwise impossible. Collaboration in groups is facilitated by noting interesting ideas or contributions, by asking what others think, by highlighting the impact that one member has on another, and by the simple act of engaging members in group problem-solving.

Adaptability and a Sense of Humor

Group process almost never progresses in a linear fashion. Like the human breathing function, groups sometimes contract and sometimes expand. Sometimes there is a focused clarity, and sometimes useful avenues of investigation get lost in distraction. Sometimes groups must dedicate a certain seriousness of intent to their interactions only to later relieve that seriousness with humor. Although openness and honesty are important, so are timing and tact.

Similarly, group leaders must sometimes "go with the flow," and sometimes redirect the process into more useful and productive activities. Adapting to the needs of the situation is not just an option in groups: It is a necessity. Once established as a group, members will always have more influence on process, direction, and movement than the leader. Leaders who are good at what systems therapists call *joining*, who participate in shared humor, who adapt and do not take themselves too seriously generally fare better and have more stamina (Corey & Corey, 2002).

Listening Teleologically

What distinguishes Adlerian group leaders from other counselors and therapists is a dedication to a psychological understanding of purpose and motive. Adlerians accept that any problem description is the individual's first attempt to make sense out of experience. "I can't talk to my parents" says something about feeling stuck and the perceived inaccessibility of parents. Nothing corrective happens at this level. When the counselor asks for a specific example, the general description is transformed into an interaction. It is in the interaction that Adlerians discover motive or purpose. We ask: "What is gained by this interchange?" If there are few socially interactive *accidents*, then what was this interaction designed to elicit or accomplish? Very often, the reaction obtained (relationally, emotionally, or behaviorally) was exactly what was sought.

A goal or a purpose makes sense out of what otherwise seems incomprehensible. Goals and purposes to which the individual attaches great significance lead to the development of patterns that reinforce both the motivation and its necessity in the person's life. Repeated patterns and motivation are always interwoven. Unlock one, and the other is merely a step away.

Holism and Working in Patterns

Adlerians believe that everything human is unified by the individual process of creating a life goal, an endpoint that envisions completion, fulfillment, actualization, and, in some cases, perfection. Every thought, feeling, behavior, and interaction can be understood as contributing to a consistent life movement or pattern. Occasionally, separate observations seem diametrically opposed to each other—even paradoxical. Dreikurs (1966) taught Adlerians to view such distinct events as *two points on a line*. It is the line that reveals the pattern.

Remember Graham from an earlier chapter? In our example, we had a man who *constantly tried to please others* on the one hand and *threw temper tantrums* on the other. What was the pattern? The line might be described in the following steps:

He offers help to someone	→	He wants appreciation but doesn't get it	→	He feels hurt	→	He decides to really do something that won't be appreciated
	→	He throws a temper tantrum to get even	→	all in the service of the life goal of *trying to please*.		

A motivation of wanting to please everyone makes sense out of all parts of his process. It also provides the counselor with a clue about how sensitive he might be to "being taken for granted" or a lack of appreciation in the group. From a teleological perspective, Adlerians might guess that there will eventually be too many people to please in his life, and he will feel pulled apart. He may fear rejection; say "yes" when he wants to say "no" (placating); and change to meet the demands of others so often that he will lose a sense of his own identity. To paraphrase Gilligan (1982), he will need help to add himself to the list of people he hopes to please.

The group setting provides a forum in which disparate actions can be reported and investigated, in which purpose can be discovered and understood. Groups also support numerous interactions in which the pattern can be enacted as well as a place for a safe experimentation with new options and different approaches.

Tending the Group Process

Ultimately, the group counselor must believe in the usefulness and dependability of the group process. There are times when, as leader, the counselor will let a possible intervention pass in the service of building or maintaining the group. Sometimes modeling, member participation and involvement, group cohesiveness, and establishing a democratic forum are more important than working with a particular individual. Letting an intervention pass, however, is not the same as losing track of the personal and psychological needs of individuals. Leadership requires often instantaneous decisions about what can be pursued, developed, and completed in a session and what needs time and attention at a later date.

In general, Adlerian group counselors lead each session *as if* it is the last. Although group members may initiate various interactions, leadership from the counselor is required if focus, new meanings or understandings, the generation of new possibilities, and closure are to be achieved.

SAFEGUARDS AND AGREEMENTS IN THE SERVICE OF GROUP PROCESS

Every group develops a way of being that is expressed in normative behavior (Yalom, 1995). Most of the time, norms are generated within and through the interactions between the leader and the group members. These norms guide and limit group behaviors in the multiple situations that will arise during the various sessions. Norms can be unspoken and subliminal, or they can be addressed, clarified, and made manifest.

The more significant norms are often referred to as group *rules* or *ground rules* (Corey & Corey, 2002; Gazda, 1989; Yalom, 1995). As we noted earlier, we don't use this language in groups anymore. In a democratic society, we reach *agreements* with each other. Sometimes these agreements are important enough to codify in one form or another, because they save lives or help us avoid serious damage to self, others, or property (e.g., traffic codes).

Although it has been noted that group leaders, by the nature of their experience and skill, have significant influence in the shaping of a group culture and group norms (Yalom, 1995), an Adlerian leader can also choose to facilitate the development of group agreements in a manner that empowers members to initiate and establish necessary guidelines.

It is not uncommon for us to initiate a discussion of group agreements, but it is the group's responsibility to reach the agreements. The content developed by group members is always important and must be respected, but the process also brings the group together and establishes a foundation for a democratic atmosphere (see chaps. 1 and 2). A typical set of agreements will protect the basic rights of individuals and enhance the flow of interaction among group members. To be effective, the number of agreements established should be rather small, and they should be stated and defined clearly.

A few agreements seem to surface more often than others. (a) Members may talk freely about anything they wish, but they must also respect the rights of others to talk freely. As far as we are concerned, this agreement includes the individual's right *not to talk* and not to be forced to talk. (b) All group discussions are confidential. It is wise to note that confidentiality is the avoidance of interactions outside the group that would either disclose names or group concerns in a manner that would hurt or embarrass other members. This agreement is different than keeping either the group or group discussion topics secret. It calls on each member to do no harm, to use her or his moral judgment to keep the interests, welfare, and privacy of others safe. (c) Members must agree to attend group sessions regularly. Needless to say, scheduled meeting times are required for implementation of this agreement. Group members may also discuss and reach agreements about what will happen if someone decides to leave the group; whether the group is open or closed; and frequency and length of group sessions.

ETHICAL CONSIDERATIONS

Ethics, as a discipline, used to address *virtue* and what constituted living a good life (see Aristotle, 1985, or Cicero, 1991). There have been a few good attempts from other fields at reintroducing this discussion into modern life (Bellah, Madsen, Sullivan, Swindler, & Tipton, 1985; Bellah, Madsen, Sullivan, Swindler, & Tipton, 1991). Counseling and psychology are disciplines/professions directly related to human functioning and the human condition. And yet, they have developed *codes of ethics* (see Corey, Corey, & Callanan, 2003) that almost completely avoid topics related to *goodness, decency, value,* and *quality* in human life. Indeed, it is a stretch to call these documents "ethical codes" at all: They have become regulations for professional practice, designed, essentially, to avoid malpractice (see Austin, Moline, & Williams, 1990).

After the devastation of World War I, Adler (1927/1957, 1938) introduced the concept of *gemeinschaftsgefuehl*: the feeling of being connected to all of humanity—past, present, and future—and to an interest in the welfare and interests of others. Adler believed that this connecting, community feeling was innate, and when developed, it would be expressed in an active social interest. *Gemeinschaftsgefuehl* is the antidote to social isolation, self-absorption, undue personal concerns, and even clinical and personality disorders. It enables courage, optimism, and ultimately confidence. People with social interest feel that they belong, that they have a place in this world and in the flow of history (Dreikurs, 1950/1953). They have a sense of humor and cope with life's demands more evenly (Bitter & West, 1979).

Furtmuller's (1964/1979), in his 1946 essay on Adler, discussed the relationship of social interest to ethics and mental health:

> The concept of social interest itself changed in character. When Adler first introduced the idea into his theory, it was a biological fact, the preparedness of the individual from the first moments of his (sic) life to establish contacts, cooperating contacts, with other individuals. Now social interest became the mentally healthy direction for the innate striving toward perfection[4]—for the individual as well as for (hu)mankind as a whole. Adler was fully aware that by this new definition social interest has left the borders of biology and entered metaphysics.[5]
>
> One reason which led Adler to this development was that undoubtedly it is impossible to be a psychotherapist without offering the patient some guidance based on ethical principles. The guidance may seemingly be completely away from ethics; for example: "Follow your drives without inner inhibitions, only be careful to avoid dangerous conflicts with established laws or customs." Such guidance may be based on ethical nihilism, but that is also a philosophy. For the Individual Psychologist it will be clear that guidance must lead along the path of cooperation.
>
> But that was not all. Individual Psychology had shown that in neurosis all the different activities of the individual become directed toward one over-all goal—fantastic personal superiority. It was only natural that the treatment should invite the individual to change his neurotic goal into one leading to the "useful side of life." This was concurrent with the theoretical position of Individual Psychology, which always had put special accent on the teleological character of all psychic activity.
>
> As an ethical principle, metaphysical social interest or related conceptions are at the root of many ethical systems and

religious creeds. That the underdevelopment of the innate potentiality for social interest, largely because of compensatory reactions against inferiority feelings, leads away from mental health is an insight for which we are indebted to Adler alone. (pp. 388–389)

Anything that can be *used* can be *misused*. This applies to group process as well as most other activities in the helping professions. For 30 years, we have known that some group experiences can negatively affect participants, and that such a result is almost always directly related to the group leader's handling of group process (Lieberman, Yalom, & Miles, 1973). Gazda (1971) reported a case in which a group leader allowed an abusive situation, resulting in the psychotic decompensation of a group member. Group leadership founded on social interest and a teleological perspective largely precludes such misuse of group process.

Certain safeguards in Adlerian group counseling and therapy help to ensure ethical practice. Although the leader listens to and acknowledges member contributions (thoughts, values, convictions, feelings, behaviors, and interactions), the focus is on the discovery of motivation and understanding personal lifestyle. One level of human expression is not elevated over another; instead, the leader urges the group to see how everything fits together in a pattern.

With the exception of parent study groups and family education centers, advice and recommendations are not dispensed. Options are generated and considered, but it is up to each member to take what fits and let go of the rest.

A certain level of openness is required for groups to work, but members are encouraged to participate in their own way—even if that way is in silent listening. In general, group members might be encouraged to be somewhat more expressive (self-disclosing) than usual if the group feels safe, and to reflect upon the meaning of the experience afterward (Lieberman et al., 1973). Honesty is also important, but it must conform to the requirements of social interest, especially in relation to offering feedback; that is, honesty must be tempered with tact and timing.

When Adlerian group counselors or therapists engage in confrontation or offer a psychological disclosure, it always comes in the form of a supposition, prefaced with "Do you think perhaps ... " "Could it be ..." or "I get the impression that ..." This tentativeness protects the group member from personal attack or extreme pressure, as well as minimizing or eliminating any form of ego destruction. It also provides a model for mutual respect in an atmosphere of social equality.

The *Ethical Guidelines for Group Counselors* (Association for Specialists in Group Work, 1989) recommends screening (when it is accepted practice within a given theoretical model); this notation allows Adlerians to accept all people who seek voluntary entrance to the group. Unfortunately, when the American Counseling Association (1995) incorporated group work into its most recent code, no such theoretical exception was noted. Indeed, the codified standards specifically mandate screening, one purpose (among others) being to ensure that no member will impede group process. Hopefully, future revision of these standards will note a legitimate Adlerian objection to a screening process and will insert a notation regarding theory similar to that in the ASGW standards.

CONCLUSION

In this chapter, we have reviewed the essential theory that supports the practice of Adlerian group counseling and therapy. The Adlerian emphasis on understanding the individual within her or his social milieu is fully realized in a group setting. In a group, members interact with peers living out the human experience. Differences in that living, whether personal or due to culture or gender, create options for consideration and make the appreciation of uniqueness possible. Group acceptance (finding a place) is therapeutic in and of itself.

Further, the group is a means of gaining insight and understanding one's problems through direct intervention or by listening to the discussions of others. Personal actions or interactions become understood, meaningful, and perhaps integrated. Learning makes change possible; the group is a safe place in which to try out new possibilities. In this sense, the group experience not only helps an individual member but also evokes a desire in that member to help others. Groups invest social interaction with real meaning. With the guidance of an experienced leader, the group becomes an agent for the formation of positive (socially useful) values and norms.

We also indicated in this chapter how we address the logistics of group practice based on our years of experience. Included in this discussion were considerations for the selection of group members; group composition; group size; group settings; and frequency, length, and duration of group meetings. In addition, we talked about the traits and abilities that we believe are required for the role of group leader, including the capacities for presence; assertiveness and confidence; courage and risk; acceptance, interest, and caring; modeling and collaboration; adaptability and a sense of humor; listening teleologically; working in holistic patterns; and tending the group process.

We concluded this chapter with a consideration of necessary safeguards for the integrity of group process and a consideration of community feeling and social interest as a foundation for ethical practice in group counseling and therapy. More than any other chapter in this book, we believe that Adlerian group leaders are defined by their ability to integrate the material we have presented here.

REFERENCES

Adler, A. (1931). *What life should mean to you* (A. Porter, Trans.). Boston: Little, Brown.
Adler, A. (1938). *Social interest: A challenge to mankind* (J. Linton & R. Vaughan, Trans.). London: Faber & Faber.
Adler, A. (1957). *Understanding human nature* (W. B. Wolfe, Trans.). New York: Premier. (Original work published 1927)
Adler, A. (1959). *The practice and theory of individual psychology: Introductory lectures in psychotherapy for physicians, psychologists, and educators* (P. Radin, Trans.). Paterson, NJ: Littlefield, Adams. (Original work published 1920)
Adler, A. (1972). *The neurotic constitution: Outlines of a comparative individualistic psychology and psychotherapy* (B. Glueck & J. E. Lind, Trans.). Freeport, MA: Books for Libraries Press. (Original work published 1926)
Adler, A. (1996a). The structure of neurosis. *Individual Psychology, 52*(4), 351–362. (Original work published 1935)
Adler, A. (1996b). What is neurosis. *Individual Psychology, 52*(4), 318–333. (Original work published 1935)
American Counseling Association. (1995). *Code of ethics and standards of practice*. Alexandria, VA: Author.
Andersen, T. (Ed.). (1991). *The reflecting team: Dialogues and dialogues about the dialogues*. New York: Norton.
Ansbacher, H. L. (1992). Alfred Adler's concepts of community feeling and social interest and the relevance of community feeling for old age. *Individual Psychology, 48*(4), 402–412.
Ansbacher. H. L., & Ansbacher, R. R. (Eds.). (1956). *The individual psychology of Alfred Adler*. New York: Basic Books.
Ansbacher, H. L., & Ansbacher, R. R. (Eds.). (1978). *Cooperation between the sexes: Writings on women, love and marriage, sexuality and its disorders*. New York: Doubleday.

Ansbacher, H. L., & Ansbacher, R. R. (Eds.). (1979). *Alfred Adler: Superiority and social interest: A collection of later writings* (3rd ed.). New York: Norton. (Original work published 1964)

Aristotle. (1985). *Nicomachean ethics* (T. Irwin, Trans.). Indianapolis, IN: Hackett.

Association for Specialists in Group Work. (1989). *Ethical guidelines for group counselors*. Alexandria, VA: Author.

Austin, K. M., Moline, M. E., & Williams, G. T. (1990). *Confronting malpractice: Legal and ethical dilemmas in psychotherapy*. Newbury Park, CA: Sage.

Bellah, R. N., Madsen, R., Sullivan, W. M., Swindler, A., & Tipton, S. M. (1985). *Habits of the heart: Individualism and commitment in American life*. New York: Harper & Row.

Bellah, R. N., Madsen, R., Sullivan, W. M., Swindler, A., & Tipton, S. M. (1991). *The good society*. New York: Alfred A. Knopf.

Bitter, J. R. (1991). Conscious motivations: An enhancement to Dreikurs' goals of children's misbehavior. *Individual Psychology, 47*(2), 210–221.

Bitter, J. R., & West, J. (1979). An interview with Heinz Ansbacher. *Journal of Individual Psychology, 35*(1), 95–110.

Bronowski, J. (1973). *The ascent of man*. Boston: Little, Brown.

Christensen, O. C. (Ed.). (1993). *Adlerian family counseling* (rev. ed.). Minneapolis, MN: Educational Media.

Cicero, M. T. (1991). *On duties* (M. T. Griffin & E. M. Atkins, Trans.). Cambridge, England: Cambridge University Press.

Copleston, F. (1959). *A history of philosophy: Volume I: Greece and Rome* (rev. ed.). Westminister, MD: Newman Press.

Corey, G. (2000). *Theory and practice of group counseling* (5th ed.). Pacific Grove, CA: Brooks/Cole.

Corey, G. (2001). *Theory and practice of counseling and psychotherapy* (6th ed.). Pacific Grove, CA: Brooks/Cole.

Corey, M. S., & Corey, G. (2002). *Groups: Process and practice* (6th ed.). Pacific Grove, CA: Brooks/Cole.

Corey, M. S., & Corey, G. (2003). *Becoming a helper* (4th ed.). Pacific Grove, CA: Brooks/Cole.

Corey, G., Corey, M. S., & Callanan, P. (2003). *Issues and ethics in the helping professions* (6th ed.). Pacific Grove, CA: Brooks/Cole.

Corsini, R. J. (1957). *Methods of group psychotherapy*. New York: McGraw-Hill.

Dinkmeyer, Jr., D., & Carlson, J. (2001). *Consultation: Creating school-based interventions*. Philadelphia: Brunner-Routledge.

Dinkmeyer, Sr., D., & Dreikurs, R. (1963). *Encouraging children to learn: The encouragement process*. Englewood Cliffs, NJ: Prentice Hall.

Dinkmeyer, D. C., & McKay, G. D. (1997). *Systematic training for effective parenting* [STEP] (rev. ed.). Circle Pines, MN: American Guidance Service.

Dreikurs, R. (1940, December). The importance of group life. *Camping Magazine, 12*, 8–9.

Dreikurs, R. (1941, January). The importance of group life. *Camping Magazine, 13,* 1.

Dreikurs, R. (1953). *Fundamentals of Adlerian psychology.* Chicago: Alfred Adler Institute. (Original work published 1950)

Dreikurs, R. (1958). *The challenge of parenthood* (rev. ed.). New York: Hawthorn. (Original work published 1948)

Dreikurs, R. (1960). *Group psychotherapy and group approaches: Collected papers.* Chicago: Alfred Adler Institute.

Dreikurs, R. (1966). The holistic approach: Two points on a line. In *Education, guidance and psychodynamics: Proceedings of the conference of the Individual Psychology Association of Chicago, St. Joseph's Hospital, November 13, 1965* (pp. 19–24). Chicago: Alfred Adler Institute.

Dreikurs, R. (1967). *Psychodynamics, psychotherapy, and counseling: Collected papers.* Chicago: Alfred Adler Institute.

Dreikurs, R. (1970). The courage to be imperfect. In Alfred Adler Institute (Ed.), *Articles of supplementary reading for parents* (pp. 17–25). Chicago: Author.

Dreikurs, R. (1971). *Social equality: The challenge of today.* Chicago: Henry Regnery. (Original work published 1961)

Dreikurs, R. (1997). Holistic Medicine. *Individual Psychology, 53*(2), 127–205.

Dreikurs, R., Corsini, R., Lowe, R., & Sonstegard, M. A. (1959). *Adlerian family counseling: A manual for counselors.* Eugene, OR: University of Oregon Press.

Dreikurs, R., & Soltz, V. (1964). *Children: The challenge.* New York: Hawthorn.

Furtmuller, C. (1979). Alfred Adler: A biographical essay. In H. L. Ansbacher & R. R. Ansbacher (Eds.), *Alfred Adler: Superiority and social interest: A collection of later writings* (3rd ed., pp. 330–394). New York: Norton. (Original work published 1964)

Gay, P. (Ed.). (1989). *The Freud reader.* New York: Norton.

Gazda, G. (1971). *Group counseling: A developmental approach.* Boston: Allyn & Bacon.

Gazda, G. (1989). *Group counseling: A developmental approach* (4th ed.). Needham Heights, MA: Allyn and Bacon.

Gilligan, C. (1982). *In a different voice: Psychological theory and women's development.* Cambridge, MA: Harvard.

Goldberger, N. R., Tarule, J. M., Clinchy, B. M., & Belenky, M. F. (Eds.). (1996). *Knowledge, difference, and power: Essays inspired by* Women's ways of knowing. New York: Basic Books.

Gottman, J. (1997). *The heart of parenting.* New York: Simon & Schuster.

Hart, B., & Risley, T. R. (1995). *Meaningful differences in the everyday experiences of young American children.* Baltimore, MD: Paul H. Brookes.

Hoffman, E. (1994). *The drive for self: Alfred Adler and the founding of individual psychology.* Reading, MA: Addison Wesley.

Kfir, N. (1981). Impasse/priority therapy. In R. J. Corsini (Ed.), *Handbook of innovative psychotherapies* (pp. 401–415). New York: Wiley.

Kirschenbaum, H., & Henderson, V. L. (Eds.). (1989). *The Carl Rogers reader.* Boston: Houghton-Mifflin.

Lieberman, M. A., Yalom, I. D., & Miles, M. B. (1973). *Encounter groups: First facts.* New York: Basic Books.

Manaster, G., & Corsini, R. J. (1982). *Individual psychology: Theory and practice.* Itasca, IL: F. E. Peacock.

Maslow, A. H. (1987). *Motivation and personality* (3rd ed.) (R. Frager, J. Fadiman, C. McReynolds, & R. Cox, Eds.). New York: Harper & Row. (Original work published 1954)

Mozdzierz, G. J., Lisiecki, J., Bitter, J. R., & Williams, A. L. (1986). Role-functions for Adlerian therapists. *Individual Psychology, 42*(2), 154–177.

Ohlsen, M. (1977). *Group counseling* (2nd ed.). New York: Holt, Rinehart, & Winston.

Polster, E. (1995). *A population of selves: A therapeutic exploration of personal diversity.* San Francisco: Jossey-Bass.

Polster, E., & Polster, M. (1973). *Gestalt therapy integrated: Contours of theory and practice.* New York: Vintage.

Popkin, M. H. (1993). *Active parenting today.* Atlanta, GA: Active Parenting.

Ratay, J. J. (2001). *A user's guide to the brain: Perception, attention, and the four theaters of the brain.* New York: Pantheon.

Satir, V. M. (1983). *Conjoint family therapy* (3rd ed.). Palo Alto, CA: Science and Behavior Books.

Satir, V. M., Bitter, J. R., & Krestensen, K. K. (1988). Family reconstruction: The family within—A group experience. *Journal for Specialists in Group Work, 13*(4), 200–208.

Schoenaker, T., & Schoenaker, T. (1975). *Adlerian social therapy* (W. L. Pew, Ed.). Minneapolis, MN: Green Bough.

Sonstegard, M. A. (1998a). A rationale for group counseling. *Journal of Individual Psychology, 54*(2), 164–175.

Sonstegard, M. A. (1998b). The theory and practice of Adlerian group counseling and psychotherapy. *Journal of Individual Psychology, 54*(2), 217–250.

Sonstegard, M. A., Dreikurs, R., & Bitter, J. (1982). The teleoanalytic group counseling approach. In G. Gazda (Ed.), *Basic approaches to group psychotherapy and group counseling* (3rd ed., pp. 507–551). Springfield, IL: Charles C. Thomas.

Sweeney, T. J. (1998). *Adlerian counseling: A practitioner's approach* (4th ed.). Philadephia, PA: Accelerated Development.

Terner, J., & Pew, W. L. (1978). *The courage to be imperfect: The life and work of Rudolf Dreikurs.* New York: Hawthorn.

Vaihinger, H. (1968). *The philosophy of "as if": A system of theoretical, practical, and religious fictions of mankind.* New York: Barnes & Noble. (Original work published 1924)

Wattenburg, W. (1953). Who needs counseling? *Personnel and Guidance Journal, 32,* 202–205.

Yalom, I. D. (1995). *The theory and practice of group psychotherapy* (4th ed.). New York: Basic Books.

NOTES

1. This chapter appeared in a different form in Sonstegard, M. A. (1998b), The theory and practice of Adlerian group counseling and psychotherapy. *Journal of Individual Psychology*, 54(2), 217–250. Reprinted with permission from University of Texas Press.
2. For a thorough presentation on Freud's theory of drives or instincts, see Gay (1989).
3. Here, the differentiation between group counseling and group therapy is not intended to suggest a significant difference in process, practice, training, or skill level of the counselor or therapist. Rather, group counseling is designated for those who are more functional and need only redirection; group therapy is indicated for those who experience themselves as more dysfunctional or in need of a restructuring of their styles of living.
4. Another word for *perfection* here might be *completion* or *actualization*.
5. The Ansbachers' footnote to Furtmuller's text reads: "Adler used the term metaphysics in the sense of ontology, as basic assumptions about man" (Ansbacher & Ansbacher, 1979, p. 389).

CHAPTER 5

Counseling Children in Groups[1]

In this chapter, we:

- Delineate the differences between group guidance, group counseling, and group therapy with children.
- Review Dreikurs' four goals of children's misbehavior as a foundation for understanding the motivations for given actions and interactions.
- Present three conscious goals for some misbehaviors in children.
- Offer a conceptualization of the mistaken notions of adults with children as a means of understanding the useless interactions that engage children and adults in seemingly unbreakable patterns.
- Consider the Adlerian stages of counseling as they directly relate to the practice of Adlerian group counseling with children.

To be human is to "live" in groups. The infant is born into a group and does not survive without the care and nurturance of others. Most children have their first group experience in a family, and the influence of that group is both substantial and critical to development (Hart & Risley, 1995). As the child grows, it moves farther and farther out—away from family (parents and siblings) into new and increasingly larger peer groups. Within family and peer groups, children gain language and voice; they create a place for themselves, define their self-worth, and discover what is possible within the boundaries of their lives. The impact of the group on each child is readily observed whenever the child participates within it.

Because the group is the reality in which children operate, those who serve them (parents, teachers, counselors, administrators, religious and community leaders) must become proficient in group process and group dynamics. Unfortunately, much of the influence that the mature could have on the immature is lost in the mistaken application of authoritarian procedures. Even at the beginning of the 21st century, we are still struggling with the negative heritage of an autocratic past. The transformation of a political democracy into a social democracy depends on the realization of social equality (Dreikurs, 1961/1971). Group counseling offers adults their best opportunity for connecting with children as social equals.

The primary concern of this chapter is group counseling with children, using the Adlerian model. Before proceeding too far, it may be useful to define some of the terminology and set the parameters for the application of this model.

DEFINITIONS

The terms *group guidance*, *group counseling*, and *group psychotherapy* are used in various ways throughout the literature (Corey, 2000; Corey & Corey, 2002; Gazda, 1989; Yalom, 1995). Although there is a considerable amount of theory and practice that overlaps in these three arenas, using these processes with children requires a more precise delineation.

Group Guidance

Although group guidance has most commonly referred to group processes enacted in schools, the practice may be properly applied by any adult who works educationally with groups of children. Group guidance includes discussions with children encouraging them to manage their own affairs or showing them how to solve the problems of everyday life. Parents, teachers, day care personnel, and other adults working with children engage in group guidance when they stimulate children to learn what *needs to be learned*—rather than merely letting them learn what they *want to learn*. Group guidance can be used to stimulate emotional structuring and growth in children, a process just as critical to human development as thinking, physical growth, and human motivation (Gottman, 1997; Gottman, Katz, & Hooven, 1997).

Many schools today have well-organized guidance programs, even in the elementary grades. School counselors have access to a variety of programs that can be used as extracurricular activities. The human development of children works best, however, when it is fully integrated into everyday life. We include here the encouragement that a teacher engenders in relationships with students while they are pursuing their everyday academic work and the stimulating manner a teacher uses to encourage the development of every child's potential. Group guidance is apparent when teachers and early childhood educators initiate cooperative and productive social climates in their classrooms; understand and work with the subgroups that are formed; and know approaches to the formation of connecting links that create integrated classrooms (Albert, 1996; Dreikurs, Grunwald, & Pepper, 1982; Popkin, 1994). Parents, too, who engage their children as a group are using group guidance procedures (for training in such interventions, see Dinkmeyer, McKay, & Dinkmeyer, 1997; Dinkmeyer, McKay, Dinkmeyer, Dinkmeyer, & McKay, 1997; Popkin, 1993, 1996).

Because many families, school systems, and other child care settings are still built on hierarchical models, often infused with authoritarian positions, adults in these settings may operate from mistaken notions with children, a concept we delineate later. Because adult mistaken notions often interlock with children's mistaken goals, creating interactive patterns that seem hard to stop, it is important for those who do group guidance and consultation (see Dinkmeyer & Carlson, 2001) to attune to and redirect the mistakes of adults as well as children.

Group Counseling

Much of what is used in group guidance can also be employed in group counseling. The differences between the two are primarily in numbers and focus: Group counseling occurs usually with small groups of 5 to 10 members; Adlerian group counseling places an emphasis on the redirection of mistaken goals and, therefore, on a motivational change in the members of the group. The group process proceeds from forming a group relationship to the uncovering and interpretation of goals, ending with efforts at reeducation (Dreikurs, 1950/1953, 1960; also see chaps. 3 and 4). Because so much of early human life is spent in groups, group counseling is the treatment of choice for most children and adolescents. The Adlerian or teleoanalytic approach with children is the subject of the rest of this chapter.

Group Therapy

Group counseling, group psychotherapy, and group therapy are often used interchangeably. When they are, the process, focus, and outcome in the Adlerian model are the same.

We are living in a world, however, where too many children are severely abused or grow up in dire poverty, exposed to drugs, guns, life-threatening violence, and death. It should not surprise us that some of these children suffer from "posttraumatic stress disorder" (American Psychiatric Association [APA], 2000, p. 463) or, conversely, join gangs for protection and to feel an artificial and negative "sense of belonging." Too many of the latter will eventually meet the criteria for what is called a "conduct disorder" (APA, 2000, p. 93). They may have already killed someone by the time they are 10, lost a major part of their soul and removed themselves in some fundamental way from humanity. They do not expect to live into adulthood. Both their immediate goals and their styles of living are dedicated to the useless and destructive side of life.

These children, when called back from the brink, often require a restructuring of personality, a complete change in lifestyle. Group process can be an effective part of the help offered. In these circumstances, the group interventions and process will be more complex, and a positive outcome usually takes longer. The terms *group therapy* and *group psychotherapy*, in these cases, distinguish the process from group counseling, not due to the skill or training of the leader, but because of the history, pain, and level of difficulties experienced by the members.

We want to emphasize here that not all difficulties currently labeled as childhood disorders in the *DSM–IV–TR* (APA, 2000) constitute a requirement for personality restructuring. Indeed, many of the disorders listed for childhood (or as beginning in childhood) are difficulties that used to be absorbed as part of everyday life. Perhaps the biggest example of this is the emphasis that is currently placed on attention deficit disorder (ADD) or attention deficit hyperactivity disorder (ADHD). There have always been children who have had difficulties with attention or who were extremely active and in constant motion. And there have always been some parents and teachers who knew how to raise such children, but also many who didn't. It's just that 50 years ago these children were not labeled with a psychiatric disorder, and they were not overly medicated—as they are today, in our opinion. We said of these children that they had trouble "paying attention" or that they had "ants in their pants."

We believe that many children currently labeled with this disorder suffer more from poor relationships with adults—deficits in the home and school—than from poor wiring in the brain or an imbalance of chemicals (see Glasser, 2003). The rate at which we are drugging our children with Ritalin and Prozac is alarming. In our experience, most of the children labeled with this psychiatric disorder do not need to be on medication at all and would benefit greatly from family counseling, involvement in a school consultation process, *and* group counseling as a regular feature of their education. In any case, such children rarely need to be in a group therapy experience designed to restructure their style of living except perhaps when violence or abuse have also been part of their early life experiences.

BASIC PRINCIPLES

Basic to the teleoanalytic group counseling approach is the formulation of a new concept of children—and humanity in general. We are not yet two centuries away from a time when unwanted female children might be killed or put on the side of a road, left to die. In the early part of the 20th century, John Watson wrote the most popular childrearing book of its day, based largely on the idea that the methods proven successful in the training of animals could be applied to the behavioral control of children (Hoffman, 1994). Adler's (1930) conceptualization removed the child, and hence all individuals, from the control of drives, urges, emotions, or even the environment; he described the child as *a growing person* who could only be understood from the perspective of the total field in which she or he, *as a human being*, operates. Child development, developmental psychology, and systems theory have only operationalized this perspective in the last 70 years.

The fields in which children operate are social (the family and one's peer group), making the primary human concern the *need to belong*, to find and hold a place with significant others (Dreikurs, 1948/1958). In finding a place, the child must be given every opportunity to utilize her or his potential to the fullest degree. If the child, however, fails to find a valued place or cannot measure up, feelings of inadequacy form the basis for retreat and may lead to maladjustment. Adlerians believe that every action of a human organism is directed toward something desired, a goal one struggles to attain (Dreikurs, 1967). The purpose of a child's behavior is always related to her or his perceived position within the social field.

Pattern and Purpose

Children are actors as well as reactors. They create the goals toward which they move. Movement toward basic goals can be seen in children as young as 2 years of age. As the child grows older, we may properly speak of two goal formations: those that are immediate and observable in day-to-day living and those that aim toward completion or perfection, the long-range, overriding goals that unify movement and eventually motivate a strategy of living.

Group counseling with children works with patterns that manifest themselves even in the fairly young. For example, a child tells an elementary counselor that his mother does not love him. He has a little brother, 4 years younger, who is very ill and requires much of his parents' time and attention. He observes that they have less time for him now; to him, this means that he is not loved. And even though his parents will claim to love both children equally, he feels displaced and begins to feel sorry for himself. Anything the parents do to indicate affection for him fails to register. He focuses only on those actions that suggest their dislike for him, actions that may simply be "provoked reactions." His private logic declares that "life is unfair." He does not realize his true intentions: to keep his parents busy, to defeat them, or to get even for having been unfairly dethroned.

Group counseling with children is concerned with immediate goals, with changes in the child's immediate behavior and the motivations that account for that behavior. Children are seldom aware of their goals unless the motivations are disclosed. Children are parsimonious: They screen out everything except what they want to learn, what they want to hear, what they need at a moment in time. A lack of goal awareness actually facilitates movement and fluidity of action; it safeguards the child from having to consciously confront the uselessness of certain behaviors.

Dreikurs' Four Goals

Dreikurs (1940) first presented his four goals of children's misbehavior as motivations for immediate problem behaviors. The four goals, *attention-getting, power struggle, revenge,* and *assumed disability* (or *demonstration of inadequacy*), described and explained early childhood patterns at least through pre-adolescence. For more than 50 years, the value of these goals has been demonstrated in parent education (Dinkmeyer, McKay, & Dinkmeyer, 1997; Dinkmeyer, McKay, Dinkmeyer, Dinkmeyer, & McKay, 1997; Dreikurs, 1948/1958; Dreikurs & Soltz, 1964; Popkin, 1993, 1996), teacher training programs (Albert, 1996; Dreikurs, 1957; Dreikurs, Grunwald, & Pepper, 1982; Popkin, 1994), consultation (Dinkmeyer & Carlson, 2001), and the training of family counselors and therapists (Christensen, 1993; Dreikurs, Corsini, Lowe, & Sonstegard, 1959; Grunwald & McAbee, 1985; Lowe, 1982).

Dreikurs (1957, 1948/1958) developed a heuristic model to delineate his four goals. The descriptions in his chart (Table 5.1) also served as one avenue for discovering the purposes of children's misbehavior.

Table 5.1
Dreikurs' Four Goals of Children's Misbehavior

Types of Behavior Pattern				Dreikurs' Four Goals
Useful Constructive		Useless Destructive		
Active	Passive	Active	Passive	
Successful Model Child	Charming Cute, Quiet	Pest Nuisance	Lazy Slow	Attention Getting
		Rebellious Argues/Says "No!"	Stubborn Passive-Aggressive	Power Struggle
		Vicious/Mean Violent	Violent Passivity	Revenge
			Hopeless	Demonstration of Inadequacy or Assumed Disability

= dots along path
--- a --- = path of active child toward increased discouragement
--- b --- = path of passive child toward increased discouragement
--- c --- = alternative path of passive child toward increased discouragement

Using Dreikurs' chart, it is possible to observe the actions of children, especially in group, and fit behaviors and interactions to possible desired outcomes. This same process can be used to understand a child's description of interactions that have taken place outside of the group—at home, in school, or with peers. Adlerians simply start any hypothesis by asking themselves, "Which of these goals could motivate a given behavior?"

Although children sometimes seek attention, power, or revenge in relation to their peers, most of the time these mistaken goals are expressed in interactions with significant adults (e.g., parents, teachers, child care personnel, etc.). In part, this is because significant adults represent "survival" beings for children in large systems. Further, adults more consistently react to provocations by children, creating a sense of familiarity and dependability (even in mistaken interactions).

Dreikurs' conceptualization of attention getting suggests that even positive behaviors can be used for this purpose. A young child might receive some positive recognition from a teacher for some effort or achievement, and then devote many interactions to reproducing that which earned him or her the initial attention. For example, Ms. Preston, a kindergarten teacher, notes that Brittany is coloring quietly, and she says, "My, what a lovely green forest." Brittany does not miss the hint. She immediately produces dozens of pretty green forests and takes every one to Ms. Preston to see how she likes the next one.

Schools in the United States, Europe, and parts of Asia are increasingly filled with children—even in the early grades—who feel that they must achieve (get straight As with reports of model behavior) just to have a place and gain the attention and recognition they need from parents and teachers. They confuse *being* the best with *trying to do* their best.

We also find many children who get attention simply for being cute or charming. If looks don't get them by, then cute and clever remarks made at just the right time seem to suffice. Some children actually become valued as "the quiet one," and especially when they are the youngest in the family, they may even be called a "prince" or "princess."

Children also use less positive behaviors to gain attention: interruptions (sometimes humorous from class clowns), wandering and other off-task behaviors, deafness to the requirements of parents and teachers, forgetfulness, poor grades, laziness, bickering, and picking fights with siblings or classmates, to name a few. Behaviors that get adults to interrupt their plans or process, to correct children, or to remind and coax—all of these actions produce the negative attention that children sometimes seek.

Similarly, power struggles signal that children are feeling one-down, that they only count if they get their own way, become the boss, or resist controlling efforts by adults. Arguments, fights, stubbornness, challenges to authority, refusals to cooperate, and work on assignments are just a few of the most common ways in which children seek and assert power. The greatest difficulty is not that a child uses these behaviors for the purpose of power, but rather that adults rarely ignore or back away from the challenge. In the end, the only way for an adult to "win" a power struggle with a child is to not get into one in the first place.

Children who *feel* hurt in their interactions with others will often seek the third of Dreikurs' goals, revenge. We emphasize the word *feel* because it is the child's interpretation of hurt that counts. Sometimes, there need be nothing to have actually provoked this feeling. Revenge can be direct: Small children may call people names, kick, or bite for revenge, whereas older children may make up lies about someone, steal, or enact some form of violent or vicious behavior. Revenge can also be indirect as in clandestine vandalism or accidentally ruining the work of another. The motive of revenge always signals a child who feels hurt and displaced.

Twenty-five years ago, children who sought to demonstrate inadequacy so that they would be left alone were hard to find. Not so today. As discouragement in children increases, parents, teachers, and counselors will see more and more children ready to give up. They may all but disappear in the classroom. They may become lethargic and even depressed. They come to believe that it is better for them not to try than to try and fail. Children who seek to become assumed disabilities are often the ones who resist or are excluded from group counseling. And they are the children who need it the most.

In addition to assessing behaviors for intended purposes, two other observations, involving adult–child interaction, can also lead the counselor to an accurate guess about a child's goal: (a) the adult's reaction to the child's misbehavior and (b) what the child does when corrected. Dreikurs and Soltz (1964) noted that adults often feel/react, predictably and on cue, in line with children's mistaken goals. Similarly, children's reactions to adult interventions also consistently reveal goals. Table 5.2 lists the observed behaviors and adult–child reactions associated with each goal.

Table 5.2
Identifying the Mistaken Goals of Children's Misbehavior

Mistaken goals	Observed behavior	What the child does when corrected	Adult response	The change process
Attention getting	Model child Charming Pest Nuisance Lazy	Stops for a short period even just a few minutes	Perhaps initially pleased with "good" behavior; then irritated annoyed or frustrated	Do the unexpected Avoid undue attention Take time for training Change the situation
Power struggle	Rebellious Argues Fights Stubborn Passive–aggressive	Keeps going with the misbehavior May intensify misbehavior	Angry Challenged Defeated	Sidestep all power struggles Act, don't talk Set limits and stick to them
Revenge	Viciousness Violence Vandalism Meanness Violent passivity	Intensifies misbehavior Misbehavior becomes mean	Hurt	Stop training and focus on relationship Encourage strengths Return friendship for hurt
Demonstration of inadequacy or Assumed disability	Acts hopeless Gives up	Limited or no interaction	Despair Helplessness	Encourage any positive behavior or movement Change the atmosphere and enjoy the child as she or he is

Dreikurs remarkable approach to goal recognition and disclosure gave counselors access to the largely unconscious motivations in children (Lowe, 1971). When an adult feels irritated or annoyed and a child stops a misbehavior after correction, even if she or he stops for just a short period of time, the counselor suspects the goal is attention getting. When adults feel angry, challenged, or defeated and the child maintains or increases the misbehavior when corrected, the goal is probably to engage adults in a power struggle. When adults feel hurt and the misbehavior intensifies after correction, becoming mean-spirited, the goal is revenge. And when children and adults both give up in despair, the child has become an assumed disability seeking to be left alone.

By carefully investigating specific interactions (i.e., what the child does, what the adult does, and what the child does in response) and noting what the adult or child is feeling in the midst of the interaction, Adlerians are able to discover the mistaken goals involved. This goal recognition process with children structures and systematizes both group and family counseling formats when children are involved. Specific examples, behavioral descriptions, and the interactions involved are central to psychological investigations and allow the counselor to form a clear picture of childhood teleology. When mistaken goals are recognized, Dreikurs (1972) used a tentative suggesting of the goal in the child's own language to seek a recognition reflex. Adlerians still follow this three-step goal disclosure process:

"Do you know why you ...?"
"I have an idea (or a different idea). Would you like to hear it?"
"Could it be that ...?"

It is not uncommon for Adlerians to suggest all four goals to children. Examples of goal disclosures are presented later in this chapter. What made Dreikurs' approach so successful is that children will only respond with recognition to goals that fit them. It is as if the child recognizes that the counselor knows that the child knows.

Conscious Goals

Based on an earlier conceptualization developed by Ansbacher (1988), I (Jim) formulated three additional goals for childhood misbehavior that I believed were complementary to Dreikurs' four goals. I call the goals *getting, self-elevation,* and *avoidance.* Like Dreikurs' more nonconscious goals, I considered these three goals to be immediate, but substantially more conscious. "It is as if the child's behavior is facilitated by knowing the purpose and making an active choice to seek it" (Bitter, 1991, p. 214).

Getting, for example, motivates much of early childhood exploration. The youngster sees something and wants it. It is not about attention or power, just the desire to have what is not currently in his or her possession. When the young child is reprimanded for taking something that is inappropriate or that belongs to someone else, he or she may later "steal" it; the motivation is still *getting*, but now the child is engaged in misbehavior. It is conscious misbehavior, because no child can *steal* without knowing she or he is doing so.

We can point to similar behaviors related to the conscious goals of *self-elevation* and *avoidance*. Tattling is a way to *elevate oneself* at the expense of another; a lie that makes a child look better than she or he really is also aims at *self-elevation*. The most common goal for lying, however, is *avoidance*—usually avoidance of anticipated trouble or punishment. Just as there are occasions when one or more of Dreikurs' goals is consciously known to a given child, there are also times when a child is served by making a conscious choice and then rendering it nonconscious. Figure 5.1, however, depicts the most common conscious versus unconscious relationship between my three goals and Dreikurs' original four goals with the horizontal diameter serving as a common boundary for childhood consciousness.

Several developmental and systemic conditions increase the likelihood that conscious motivations might be involved in a child's misbehavior:

- The misbehavior is enacted by very young (preschool) children.
- The children involved have received a lot of punishment.
- The children involved have been raised by one or more adults who are excessive worriers.
- The misbehavior seems more embedded in child-to-child (especially sibling) interactions than adult–child interactions.

Because these conditions define most group counseling with children, it is not uncommon for the counselor discover conscious motivations at work. In a group of elementary school children, Ann described a temper tantrum she had thrown the night before. The counselor asked the group why Ann might have acted in that manner. After considering a number of possibilities, the counselor asked if he

Counseling Children in Groups 147

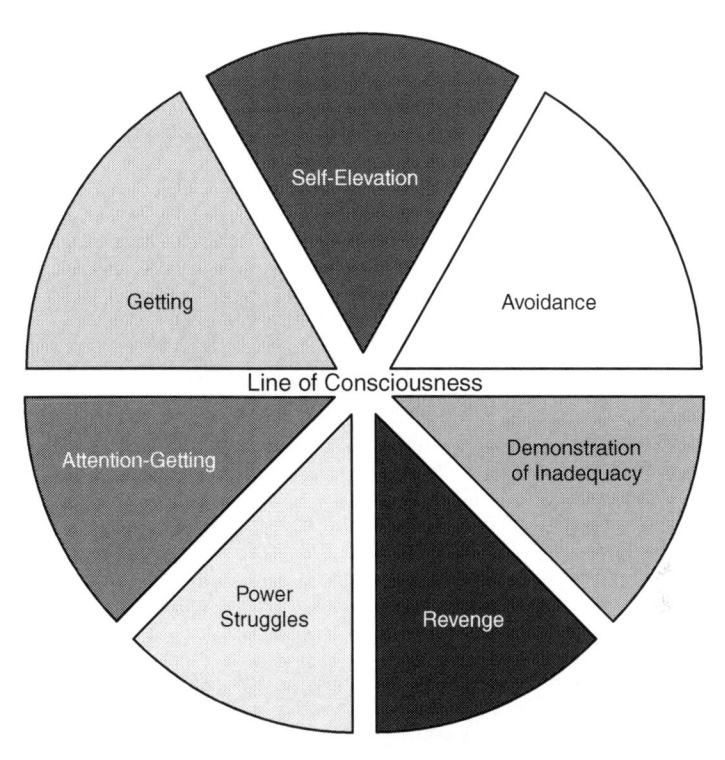

Figure 5.1 Conscious and nonconscious motivations of children's misbehavior.

could make a guess: "Perhaps you want to show your parents that you are the boss and can do whatever you please." But the intervention produced no recognition.

Another group member asked: "Did you get mad so they would give you what you wanted (the goal of *getting*)?" To this question, Ann responded with a recognition reflex—just before she said, "no." In later group interactions, Ann's goal resurfaced: She admitted that sometimes she just saw things that other people had, and she wanted to have them too, so she took them. She felt she deserved whatever other people had. Over time, she came to understand the purpose of her behaviors and to reconsider what her options were.

The Mistaken Notions of Adults With Children

The mistaken goals of children's misbehavior are always socially embedded and enacted in interactions with others. Because adults must react in predictable patterns in order to keep misbehaviors going, it is reasonable to ask, "What keeps adults from simply disengaging?" What purpose do their interactions with children have? What goals do they seek?

Dreikurs (1948/1958) first suggested that the mistaken goals of children would elicit a parallel set of mistaken goals in significant adults who had ongoing interactions with children. After all, children have little else but their family and school relationships to occupy them, and they are very skilled at studying and reading adults. Today, we can characterize the mistaken notions of adults with children as "a *demonstration of adequacy, control, revenge,* and a *demonstration of inadequacy*" (Bitter, Roberts, & Sonstegard, 2002, p. 53).

No adult becomes a parent or goes into the professions of teaching and child care with the intention of being a negative influence in a child's life. To the contrary, all adults want to demonstrate that they are "good" parents or teachers. Each was raised with or adopted certain values and beliefs that define what adults are like when they are functionally raising and educating youngsters. It is as if we adults say, "I will be good with children if they are ___ (happy, safe, polite, achievers, successful, athletic; each person fills in the blank personally)." Further, adults tend to respond to those behaviors that either reinforce their fondest dreams or challenge them. It is no accident, therefore, that children's attention-getting behaviors are almost always in direct relation to adult processes and goals for demonstrating competence, effectiveness, and *adequacy* as parents or teachers.

When adequacy in adults feels threatened, that is when most respond with lectures, excessive supervision, pampering, overprotection, spankings, restrictions, time-outs, reminding, coaxing, and nagging. Children, then, engage in negative attention getting or even power struggles.

Whether it starts with the adult or the child, power struggles and the adult goal of *control* go hand-in-hand. For some adults, control is their demonstration of adequacy. This is especially true in public schools in America. Others escalate their drive to control as children increase their power-oriented behaviors. Arguing or fighting with a child, declaring you're "the boss," defensiveness, withholding, and anger are all sure signs that an adult is losing in the battle to gain control.

Just as children can feel hurt and seek *revenge,* so can adults. Adult revenge is an especially dangerous goal because of the differential in power; it too often winds up in abusive or neglectful behaviors. Contempt, name calling, disparagement, extreme and severe punishments, rejections, and violent outbursts are all signs of the revenge goal in adults.

It is harder for adults to give up on children than for children to give up on themselves. Adults have a lot of social and legal pressure on them regarding their duties to the children they bring into the world. Still, we occasionally see some parents—and more rarely, some teachers—who become so discouraged that they merely go through the motions of child care, if they do anything. They actually want the child to go away. They demonstrate enough *inadequacy* so that others will realize they are in over their heads. They want to be left alone. They are neglectful and self-absorbed.

It is easy to see that as an adult progresses through these goals, he or she becomes increasingly discouraged, with the latter two goals signaling dangerous interactions and the need for professional interventions. Even the less discouraged positions in which the goals are a demonstration of adequacy or control, however, easily interlock with children's attention getting and power, making it difficult for either party to disengage.

No adult is totally immune from the potential for mistaken interactions with children. Any given child can push an adult "button" given enough time for study and trial and error—and enough determination. Those of us who provide group guidance and group counseling will experience numerous attempts by various youngsters to draw us into mistaken interactions. It is important, therefore, that those of us who work with children know where we are vulnerable. The values and functions of the group counselor that we outlined in the last chapter are the best antidote to reactivity. As group leaders, we seek a position that is self-controlled, encouraging, understanding, and that models empathic listening and acceptance.

Although the greatest uses of the mistaken notions of adults with children may be in family therapy or consultation with teachers, it is also a useful guide for helping children in groups understand the goals and behaviors of parents or teachers. Here is an excerpt from a group counseling session with seventh graders in a middle school. Two of the boys in the group have been complaining about a math teacher "who hates them" and with whom they are in an almost constant power struggle.

Ralph: Ole Lady Hanson is a Nazi.
Tommy: Yeah, she actually gave the class thirty extra problems for homework last night just because a few of us were talking.

Amy:	It wasn't "a few of us": It was you and Ralph. And I didn't like having to do those problems just because the two of you were goofing around.
Ralph:	Ah, she's just mean!
Amy:	I don't know. I kind of like her.
Counselor:	Why is that, Amy?
Amy:	She always has a schedule each day and for each week. I always know exactly what I have to do—providing these two don't make more work.
Counselor:	So, she's very precise.
Amy:	Yes, and she explains how to do math problems really well, step by step. I don't get lost like I did last year.
Counselor:	Ralph, Amy seems to have found some value in Ms. Hanson, but you feel there is none in her. To you and Tommy, she's just mean. Why do you think she has such trouble with the two of you?
Ralph:	Maybe because she knows we don't like her.
Counselor:	Maybe, but I have another idea: Would you like to hear it?
Tommy:	Yeah.
Ralph:	Okay.
Counselor:	Could it be that order and control are very important to Ms. Hanson. Maybe she feels lost when things get out of control, and the things that the two of you often do seem to her that the class she has carefully—even precisely—prepared is about to become chaotic.
Tommy:	Yeah, and then she tries to control us, but she can't. She'll lose every time (smiling).
Counselor:	Let me ask you something else: Can you tell when Ms. Hanson is having a bad day; you know, a worse day than normal?
Ralph:	Of course.
Counselor:	And when she is, do you ease up on her?
Ralph:	(pause) Not usually. To tell the truth, I generally try to put her away.
Amy:	And that's when we all get extra homework. (looking at the counselor) I don't even blame her for wanting to get even with them. I would want to get even too.

PHASES OF GROUP COUNSELING

The teleoanalytic approach permits certain orientations in group counseling as well as specific interpretations of observed phenomena (Dreikurs, 1960; Sonstegard & Dreikurs, 1973; Sonstegard, Dreikurs, & Bitter, 1982; chap. 4). Following an Adlerian intervention model, the counselor first works to establish a cohesive group relationship with members and between them; second, the counselor leads a psychological investigation emphasizing motivation in the understanding of children and their problems; third, the counselor facilitates revelations using the tentative goal disclosing process developed by Dreikurs (1972); fourth, the counselor initiates a reorientation, a redirection of the child's mistaken goals and the development of more useful patterns of living.

Forming a Group Relationship

The establishment of a working relationship with children in groups is more than merely having positive and congenial interactions. The group leader engages children in a manner that models mutual respect, takes into account the developmental level of the members (Gazda, 1989; Waterman & Walker, 2000), and infuses interactions with psychological meaning. Reaching agreements about everything from when the group will meet to an understanding of personal goals elicits a group relationship. Even young preschool children can engage in this process; they simply need a more active leadership and guidance.

A mutual agreement about goals is too often neglected, leading the counselor into group resistance. Even when children need and want help and the counselor wishes to be helpful, there can be a variance about how each perceives help and the means used to achieve this objective. The child may want to change, but there may be overriding factors that present as obstacles; for example, the child may be exceedingly discouraged or determined to demonstrate hopelessness (as opposed to failure). Counselors must also be prepared for children who take the same attitude toward the leader that they do with everyone else in society—often trying to defeat the counselor by provoking a power struggle. Some children also feel that they have worked out a satisfactory place in society even if that place lacks social interest or may even be antisocial.

The group, when encouraged to do so, will facilitate the cooperation necessary to the establishment of common objectives. With very discouraged youngsters, this process can take a long time, because there is not a history of trust on which to count or build. Counselors must be patient. The process of establishing and maintaining a cooperative relationship is corrective in and of itself. When children agree on immediate common goals with the counselor, their own goals and roles have already changed. It may be the first experience a child has ever had of a cooperative working relationship with an adult: the first time the child has ever participated in significant decision making. The counselor may be the child's first experience of an adult who listens, who helps the child to make sense out of personal experiences rather than representing the "authority" of society and of the adult world. If the counselor is able to convey the feeling of acceptance, understanding, and anticipation of success rather than failure, the basis for a group relationship is established.

Counselors need multiple ways of "feeling" their way into groups. Younger children often need more structure initially. The leader may find it useful to note agreements other groups have had and to ask what this group thinks of those agreements. Similarly, when young children begin to talk about their lives, they may have no idea of how to start. Again, we often tell them about topics or issues that other groups have discussed in the past. Or we may initiate a conversation in a psychologically useful manner, asking about their family constellations, some of their strengths and weaknesses, or if there is now (or ever was) something that worried them. Very young children usually need a tighter focus too: Shorter sessions are useful, ones in which an idea is developed, considered, and tentative conclusions are reached. Older children will take greater charge of the group process. In general, the leader should let the group members handle as much of the group direction and process as possible.

Psychological Investigation

Adlerian counselors actively explore the social situations (the fields of involvement) of children as well as the strategies used to cope. The first level of investigation is usually the child's *subjective* condition: the child's complaints, problems, concerns; personal reactions and feeling; and worries—or people and events that bother the youngster. Even mildly discouraged children and adolescents are less protective than most adults; they can hardly keep from expressing their stance in relation to life. The subjective interview often reveals enough material to keep a group going for weeks. An *objective* interview, the second level of investigation, explores how the individual functions in the "living" situations of one's life (i.e., home, neighborhood, and school) and how one interacts with family and peers. With older adolescents, it is even possible to conduct reasonable, if modified, lifestyle assessments (again, see Eckstein & Baruth, 1996; Powers & Griffith, 1987; Shulman & Mosak, 1988) as part of the objective interview. Adlerians have long emphasized the usefulness of family constellation, investigating parental relationship, parent–child interactions, family atmosphere, and birth order/sibling relationships in an objective interview (Bitter et al., 2002). Developmental experiences and early recollections can be used with older adolescents in developing clues about the individual's patterns of living.

As long as the counselor maintains a psychological orientation, a number of different approaches to exploration can be used. Adlerians have used play therapy, puppets, and drawings (DeOrnellas, Kottman, & Millican, 1997; Kottman, 2001, 2003; Sonnenshein-Schneider & Baird, 1980); role playing and role reversal (Kern & Eckstein, 1997; Sonnenshein-Schneider & Baird, 1980); and dream work and creative arts (Dushman & Sutherland, 1997). Any of these approaches can be effective in assessment and reorientation, if applied with an orientation to the psychological: to purposes, goals, and coping patterns. Playing with children is not the same as play therapy, any more than a group discussion is necessarily group counseling.

Interpretation

The goal of this step in the process is to reveal coping strategies and their motives: the private logic, the mistaken notions and goals, that support dysfunctional behavior. When working with relatively young children (up to about the age of 10), most interpretations and disclosures are related to the goals for misbehavior [either Dreikurs' or mine (Jim)]. Groups have an advantage over individual counseling in that the members are involved in the discussion, speculating about goals and motives, relating patterns from earlier investigations to a current problem, and addressing ideas and stances of their peers.

Children grow up in a world where it is falsely suggested that any action or effect always has a specific cause, a cause usually outside of the individual. This perspective is often reflected in group members' speculations. The counselor's focus on purpose and goals helps to make sense of experience, to develop a purposive understanding of one's actions and interactions, rather than to leave a child stuck in the reactivity of feelings.

As has already been noted, Adlerian goal disclosure with children is approached tentatively, allowing each child to consider the information and decide about its usefulness. In general, accurate interpretations and goal disclosures from members support group process better than counselor interventions. We ask even young group members to guess about possible motivations: "Why do you think John gets in fights with his sister all the time?"

Only when group members fail to produce a probable goal do we offer our thinking: "You have all suggested good possibilities, but I have an idea about this. Would you like to hear it?"

Common wording for our disclosures are listed below for each goal.

- *"Could it be that* you want to keep mom or dad busy with you?" (attention getting: Dreikurs' goal 1)
- *"Could it be that* you want to show mom or dad that you are the boss or that no one can make you stop?" (power struggle: Dreikurs' goal 2)
- *"Could it be that* you feel hurt and want to get even with mom or dad?" (revenge: Dreikurs' goal 3)
- *"Could it be that* you would like to be left alone?" (assumed disability: Dreikurs' goal 4),
- *"Could it be that* you think you should get whatever you want and you are willing to do anything to get it?" (getting: conscious goal 5)
- *"Could it be that* you want only to be the best or show people how big and important you are?" (self-elevation: conscious goal 6)
- *"Could it be that* you were worried about getting punished?" Or *"Could it be that* you didn't want to look bad or make a mistake?" (avoidance: conscious goal 7)

If the therapist is correct with any of the guesses, the child will exhibit a "recognition reflex," generally expressed in a smile and a twinkle in the eyes. It is the look that a child might have when caught with hands in a cookie jar. Regardless of the child's verbal response, the reflex is a confirmation of the diagnostic hypothesis (Bitter, 1991; Lowe, 1971). Further, even if the child says "No, that's not it," the recognition reflex suggests that the goal is now conscious and can be addressed over time in a nonthreatening manner.

Reorientation

Groups can accomplish a redirection of children without the necessity of interpretation. We know this because of the success of other approaches to counseling (e.g., person-centered therapy, gestalt therapy, reality therapy, play therapies, cognitive-behavioral therapies, and even some forms of constructivist therapies, such as narrative and solution-focused). The success of these models seems to suggest that reorientation operates on its own dynamic elements.

Adlerians consider reorientation the final and most important step in the change process, a phase in which new understandings translate into action and new options in a child's life. The more life experience group members have had, the more useful group suggested options for change are likely to be. Older children and adolescents tend to generate creative and useful options if given time. The counselor's intervention in such cases may merely be to emphasize or highlight a point: "John, what do you think about what Jean suggested?" (See chap. 2 for an example of this process.)

Most of the dynamics of reorientation can be attributed to the strength of the relationships between group members as well as between the group members and the counselor. Acceptance and understanding go a long way toward removing resistance to change. A child who sees her or his behavior as having a goal is less likely to get lost in the internalized sense of "good/bad; right/wrong" that is a constant in adult–child interactions. Options are always possible once children discover there is more than one way to reach a goal. Group counseling helps the child to become aware of the personal power in making decisions; of the freedom and responsibility involved in choosing one's own direction; and of the ability to count and be useful in the lives of others.

Encouragement is the essential factor in all reorientation and corrective efforts with children. The redirection of mistaken goals requires a restoration of the child's faith in self and a realization of strengths and abilities, dignity and worth. Without encouragement, no counseling approach will make a difference. From an earlier presentation (Sonstegard & Dreikurs, 1973), we illustrate the power of encouragement within a group counseling session with children.

> Kebb was referred to group counseling for what the teacher called "abnormal" behavior. He would expose himself in the washrooms and halls, and both teacher and principal

became very busy with surveillance. The more he was watched, the more frequent became the "abnormal" behavior .... In the group, Kebb was unresponsive, but he defended himself during a discussion [in which] one member brought up the fact that Kebb never finished his work and did not study his reading.

    Kebb: I finished it today.
    Counselor: Did you finish all of it or did you finish part of it?
    Kebb: Yeah, I ... well ... ah ... I did most of it.
    Counselor: Would you show it to us? I would be interested in what you are doing.
    Kebb: Yeah.
    Counselor: Could you show it to us now?
    Kebb: Yeah. (He left for the classroom and returned with his work and a reading book.)
    Kebb: I can read, too!
    Counselor: I am sure you can.

The written work left much to be desired, but the counselor began to point out some good things. The letters were well formed. Kebb put periods at the end of sentences and capitals at the beginning so one could read it easily. The counselor read a good part of it out loud, and the group agreed that Kebb had some good ideas. Kebb became responsive and began to give other ideas he wanted to include. ... Then Kebb enthusiastically picked up the book to read.

    Member: That's not the book we're reading in. (Kebb slumped in his seat.)
    Counselor: Does it really make a difference? (Some members agreed it really did not.)
    Kebb: I like the stories in this book better. (The book was actually an easier book.)

Kebb read fairly well, but missed some words. Again, the counselor emphasized strong points—the expression and the interpretations. Kebb felt better now and sat up in his chair. He read on with more confidence. (p. 64)

CONCLUSION

The problems with which each child struggles stem from interactions in groups, primarily family and peer groups; these problems must therefore be solved in groups. Group counseling contributes to the dissolution of the social walls within which most children live. Over a period of time, group members develop a real interest in helping others in the group. In this chapter, we have delineated the differences between group guidance, group counseling, and group therapy with children. We also noted the basic psychological issues involved in counseling children in groups, including a review of Dreikurs four goals of children's misbehavior and Jim's three conscious goals for some misbehaviors. We also looked at the mistaken notions of adults working with children and how these goals interact with children's mistaken goals to form interactive patterns that are hard to break. Finally, the four stages of Adlerian counseling (i.e., forming a relationship, a psychological investigation, psychological disclosure, and reorientation) were applied to our work with children and young adolescents in groups.

REFERENCES

Adler, A. (1930). *The education of children* (E. Jensen & F. Jensen, Trans.). New York: Greenberg.

Albert, A. (1996). *Cooperative discipline.* Circle Pines, MN: American Guidance Service.

American Psychiatric Association. (2000). *Diagnostic and statistical manual of mental disorders* (4th ed., text rev.) [*DSM–IV–TR*]. Washington, DC: Author.

Ansbacher, H. L. (1988). Dreikurs' four goals of children's disturbing behavior and Adler's social interest—activity typology. *Individual Psychology, 44*(3), 282–289.

Bitter, J. R. (1991). Conscious motivations: An enhancement to Dreikurs' goals of children's misbehavior. *Individual Psychology, 47*(2), 210–221.

Bitter, J. R., Roberts, A., & Sonstegard, M. (2002). Adlerian family therapy. In J. Carson & D. Kjos (Eds.), *Theories and strategies of family therapy* (pp. 41–79). Boston: Allyn & Bacon.

Christensen, O. C. (Ed.). (1993). *Adlerian family counseling* (rev. ed.). Minneapolis, MN: Educational Media Corp.

Corey, G. (2000). *Theory and practice of group counseling* (5th ed.). Pacific Grove, CA: Brooks/Cole.

Corey, M. S., & Corey, G. (2002). *Groups: Process and practice* (6th ed.). Pacific Grove, CA: Brooks/Cole.

DeOrnellas, K., Kottman, T., & Millican, V. (1997). Drawing a family: Art assessment in Adlerian therapy. *Individual Psychology, 53*(4), 451–460.

Dinkmeyer, D., Jr., & Carlson, J. (2001). *Consultation: Creating school-based interventions.* Philadelphia: Brunner-Routledge.

Dinkmeyer, D., Sr., McKay, G., & Dinkmeyer, D., Jr. (1997). *Systematic training for effective parenting [STEP]* (rev. ed.). Circle Pines, MN: American Guidance Service.

Dinkmeyer, D., Sr., McKay, G., Dinkmeyer, J. S., Dinkmeyer, D., Jr., & McKay, J. (1997). *Parenting young children: Systematic training for effective parenting of children under six.* Circle Pines, MN: American Guidance Service.

Dreikurs, R. (1940, December). The child in the group. *Camping Magazine,* pp. 7–9.

Dreikurs, R. (1953). *Fundamentals of Adlerian psychology.* Chicago: Alfred Adler Institute. (Original work published 1950)

Dreikurs, R. (1957). *Psychology in the classroom.* New York: Harper & Row.

Dreikurs, R. (1958). *The challenge of parenthood* (rev. ed.). New York: Hawthorn. (Original work published 1948)

Dreikurs, R. (1960). *Group psychotherapy and group approaches: Collected papers.* Chicago: Alfred Adler Institute.

Dreikurs, R. (1967). *Psychodynamics, psychotherapy, and counseling: Collected papers.* Chicago: Alfred Adler Institute.

Dreikurs, R. (1971). *Social equality: The challenge of today.* Chicago: Henry Regnery. (Original work published 1961)

Dreikurs, R. (1972). The individual psychological approach. In B. B. Wolman (Ed.), *Handbook of child psychoanalysis* (pp. 415–459). New York: Van Nostrand Reinhold.

Dreikurs, R., Corsini, R., Lowe, R., & Sonstegard, M. A. (1959). *Adlerian family counseling: A manual for counselors.* Eugene, OR: University of Oregon Press.

Dreikurs, R., Grunwald, B. B., & Pepper, F. C. (1982). *Maintaining sanity in the classroom: Classroom management techniques* (2nd ed.). New York: Harper & Row.

Dreikurs, R., & Soltz, V. (1964). *Children: The challenge.* New York: Hawthorn.

Dushman, R. D., & Sutherland, J. (1997). An Adlerian perspective on dreamwork and creative arts therapies. *Individual Psychology, 53*(4), 461–475.

Eckstein, D., & Baruth, L. (1996). *The theory and practice of lifestyle assessment.* Dubuque, IA: Kendall/Hunt.

Gazda, G. (1989). *Group counseling: A developmental approach* (4th ed.). Needham Heights, MA: Allyn & Bacon.

Glasser, W. (2003). *Warning: Psychiatry can be hazardous to your mental health.* New York: Harper/Collins.

Gottman, J. (1997). *The heart of parenting.* New York: Simon & Schuster.

Gottman, J. M., Katz, L. F., & Hooven, C. (1997). *Meta-emotion: How families communicate emotionally.* Mahwah, NJ: Lawrence Erlbaum Associates.
Grunwald, B. B., & McAbee, H. V. (1985). *Guiding the family: Practical counseling techniques.* Muncie, IN: Accelerated Development.
Hart, B., & Risley, T. R. (1995). *Meaningful differences in the everyday experiences of young American children.* Baltimore, MD: Paul H. Brookes.
Hoffman, E. (1994). *The drive for self: Alfred Adler and the founding of individual psychology.* Reading, MA: Addison Wesley.
Kern, R. M., & Eckstein, D. (1997). The early recollection role reversal technique. *Individual Psychology, 53*(4), 407–417.
Kottman, T. (2001). *Play therapy: Basics and beyond.* Alexandria, VA: American Counseling Association.
Kottman, T. (2003). *Partners in play* (2nd ed.). Alexandria, VA: American Counseling Association.
Lowe, R. N. (1971). Goal recognition. In A. G. Nikelly (Ed.), *Techniques for behavior change* (pp. 65–75). Springfield, IL: Charles C. Thomas.
Lowe, R. N. (1982). Adlerian/Dreikursian family counseling. In A. M. Horne & M. M. Ohlsen (Eds.), *Family counseling and therapy* (pp. 329–359). Itasca, IL: F. E. Peacock.
Popkin, M. H. (1993). *Active parenting today.* Atlanta, GA: Active Parenting.
Popkin, M. H. (1994). *Active teaching: Enhancing discipline, self-esteem, and student performance.* Atlanta, GA: Active Parenting.
Popkin, M. H. (1996). *Parenting your 1- to 4-year-old.* Atlanta, GA: Active Parenting.
Powers, R. L., & Griffith, J. (1987). *Understanding life-style: The psycho-clarity process.* Chicago: Americas Institute of Adlerian Studies.
Shulman, B., & Mosak, H. H. (1988). *Manual for lifestyle assessment.* Muncie, IN: Accelerated Development.
Sonnenshein-Schneider, M., & Baird, K. L. (1980). Group counseling children of divorce in the elementary schools: Understanding process and technique. *Personnel and Guidance Journal, 59*(2), 88–91.
Sonstegard, M. A., & Bitter, J. R. (1998). Counseling children in groups. *Journal of Individual Psychology, 54*(2), 251–267.
Sonstegard, M. A., & Dreikurs, R. (1973). The Adlerian approach to group counseling of children. In M. M. Ohlsen (Ed.), *Counseling children in groups: A forum* (pp. 47–77). New York: Holt, Rinehart, & Winston.
Sonstegard, M. A., Dreikurs, R., & Bitter, J. R. (1982). The teleoanalytic group counseling approach. In G. M. Gazda (Ed.), *Basic approaches to group psychotherapy and group counseling* (3rd ed., pp. 507–551). Springfield, IL: Charles C. Thomas.
Waterman, J., & Walker, E. (2000). *Helping at-risk students: A group counseling approach for grades 6-9.* New York: Guilford.
Yalom, I. D. (1995). *The theory and practice of group psychotherapy* (4th ed.). New York: Basic Books.

NOTE

1. This chapter appeared in a different form in Sonstegard, M. A. and Bitter, J. R. (1998), Counseling children in groups. *Journal of Individual Psychology*, 54(2), 251–267. Reprinted with permission from University of Texas Press.

CHAPTER 6

The Education and Training of a Group Therapist

James Robert Bitter, Peggy Pelonis, and Manford A. Sonstegard

In this chapter, we:

- Propose an ideal program for the education and training of a group therapist, including:
  - A group experience as an initial starting point.
  - Observation of group process over an extended period of time.
  - Application of group theory, process, and evaluation to personal group experience and observations.
  - Coleadership and supervision.
- Present a model based on Satir's (1976) communication stances and Kfir's (1971, 1989; Kfir & Corsini, 1981) personality priorities that can be used by group counselors and therapists to assess personal triggers as well as to understand coping processes in group experiences.
- Note the importance of journaling in the training of group counselors and therapists and how electronic media can be used to facilitate this process.
- Revisit the stages of group as they are considered during training, and propose a course process for blending theory, coleadership, and supervision.

There was a time in the medical profession when the interventions of its leading practitioners were often more detrimental than the illnesses that patients suffered. Until the turn of the last century, for example, bloodletting or "bleeding" was still a treatment of choice when serious illness was encountered. Indeed, it was this very treatment that killed George Washington after he contracted a respiratory illness. The great difficulty for the medical profession in Washington's America was (a) a limited understanding of the bodily systems and how they worked, and (b) a tendency to use a single intervention for most serious illnesses.

Thanks to a century of research and more exacting medical standards, surgical procedures today provide organ transplants and precision laser operations that could not have been imagined less than 100 years ago. Indeed, some deadly diseases, such as smallpox, have all but been eradicated from the face of the earth.

We believe that the knowledge and skills needed to understand human behavior and human motivations require at least the same amount of time and effort required to prepare a general medical practitioner. Our belief in such training is gradually being accepted in the fields of psychology, social work, and counseling, as each of these disciplines increases the coursework and time required for both terminal degrees and licensure (see guidelines for American Psychological Association [APA] programs [http://www.apa.org], the American Counseling Association [ACA] CACREP standards [http://www.counseling.org/about/orgs.htm], and National Association of Social Workers [NASW] programs [http://www.socialworkers.org]).

Counselors, social workers, and psychologists work in schools, community agencies, and managed care facilities where they regularly experience caseloads that far exceed their capabilities for offering individual therapy. Even though training in group work would seem to be one of the more expedient ways to address this difficulty, it remains one of the most underdeveloped aspects of programs for professional helpers. Both APA and CACREP credentialing personnel, for example, regularly sign off on curricula that include as little as one course in group process and 40 group contact hours suggested during practica experiences.

The kind of training program we would hope to see in university settings would begin to approach the thoroughness of clinical training in medicine and would include:

1. A group experience for all people entering the professions of counseling, social work, or psychology.

2. Observation of group process over an extended period of time.
3. Didactic training in group theory, group process, and group evaluation directly related to personal group experiences and observed processes.
4. Coleadership of groups under supervision.
5. A practicum or internship with a prominent use of group work and adequate supervision.

A GROUP EXPERIENCE FOR GRADUATE STUDENTS IN THE HELPING PROFESSIONS

In spite of the fact that students in the helping professions will ask their clients to disclose the most intimate details of their personal lives, many future counselors and therapists are often quite reluctant to share anything personal from their own experiences. The "best practices" for group counselors and group psychotherapists call for group leaders to engage in reflective practice and to review and assess their competence and preparedness for group leadership (Rapin & Keel, 1998). First group experiences—even when they are not oriented toward Adlerian practice—provide future therapists with what may be their first experiences of extended silences, shared issues and concerns, empathic understanding, personal confrontation, emotional involvement and engagement, the development of group cohesion, and the power of group support and group norms (Gladding, 2003). It is also common for these initial groups to provide participants with experiences they will meet in group work for years to come: individuals who remain quiet or monopolize, for example, or larger process issues related to race, ethnicity, and gender.

Adlerian group counseling and therapy augments these initial experiences with a focus on systemic understanding of individuals; the development of voice and effective communication (Gilligan, 1982; Satir, 1976); the impact of personality priorities during impasse or stress (Kfir, 1971, 1989; Kfir & Corsini, 1981); the investigation and understanding of lifestyle (Powers & Griffith, 1987); and the experience of community feeling and social interest (Ansbacher, 1992) within the group. In addition to contributing to the self-understanding of future group leaders and therapists, the group experience provides some clarity about the coping processes the individual is most likely to enlist under stress.

Life without problems, without difficulties and stress, is a myth. What makes us different from one another, in part, is the style and process we bring to coping. All coping precedes and anticipates desired solutions and outcomes. If I want everyone to be happy, for example, I am less likely to cope well with anger and confrontation. Or perhaps, if people express hurt, loss, or pain, I will want to "fix" them. How we communicate under stress is intimately related to how we perceive self, others, and the world, as well as to what we feel compelled to do in an effort to effectively cope with the demands of difficult situations (Bitter, 1993).

Peggy and Jim have both studied with the late pioneer of American family therapy, Virginia Satir. She developed descriptions of four communication stances that, when used, contributed to and expressed stress and dysfunctional coping—especially during the ongoing process of change that *is* life (Pelonis, 2002). Satir (1976) called these stress positions *blaming, placating, super-reasonable,* and *irrelevant.*

At roughly the same time in Israel, an Adlerian psychologist named Nira Kfir (1971, 1989) introduced the concept of personality priorities. These personality priorities represented the goals that individuals have—a first line of defense—when stress was high and people feel like they are reaching an impasse. Kfir identified four priorities: *significance* or *superiority, pleasing, control,* and *comfort.*

The relationship between Satir's communication stances and Kfir's personality priorities has been noted elsewhere (Bitter, 1987, 1993). They have a special value in the training of group counselors. Early group experiences, whether as a participant or as a leader, often include a greater sense of anxiety and stress than is present in individual therapy. Especially in cultures that discourage the sharing of personal issues outside of the family, individual therapy may be seen as more private and therefore safer. It is often individuals from these same cultures, however, that seek ongoing groups, stay with them longer, or seek multiple group experiences, once they have experienced one. In groups, there are always more people who need our attention, who have differing needs, and who form alliances. Interaction is the process of group, and the purposes and sequences of interaction are more difficult to follow than when one is merely listening to a single individual. Further, a client can choose to hide, ignore, or deny major issues when in individual therapy, but in group sessions, issues of great personal and emotional importance often surface in ways that cannot be ignored. When the stress of handling group process is high, knowing our *triggers*—the ways in which we will automatically react—is essential information.

Communication processes are often the most observable manifestation of individual coping and "triggered" responses. The following descriptions are portraits of coping processes generated from integrating Satir's communication stances during stress with Kfir's personality priorities (Table 6.1).

Placating–Pleasing

People seeking to please others will agree with whatever is said. When stress is high, those who placate are attempting to be sincerely deferential: They are willing to sacrifice themselves for the good of others. Placating–pleasing starts with low self-esteem, and only a hope that others will love them. In the extreme, people may feel worthless and find themselves saying "yes" to any request, no matter what they really think or feel. Placating–pleasing people are always a little nervous, because they do not feel effective at assessing their own actions. They easily form complementary relationships with those who blame and seek significance. Because the weight of other's happiness is always on their shoulders, their strength is in their ability to persevere, to endure. Unfortunately, people who placate–please have a lot land on them, especially in abusive relationships.

Blaming–Significance

When stress goes up, the complement to placating–pleasing is blaming and the battle to maintain significance or superiority at any cost. People in this position will sacrifice others and even the basic needs of the interpersonal context to maintain and preserve self-worth. The priority of significance–superiority depends on being one-up, highly regarded, or having power. When problems occur, fault must be assigned elsewhere. The communication is expressed in the form of disagreement and criticism of others—a stance that masks an equally strong tendency toward self-criticism. People in this position feel pressured most of the time: There is an irritation just below the surface that quickly becomes anger when challenged.

Blaming–significance people want to avoid meaninglessness and worthlessness. Their self-esteem may rest on the delicate sense of being on top, in charge, or at least blameless in the face of difficulties. There is often an almost bipolar movement between procrastination and overdoing. They may complain of being overworked and overbur-

Table 6.1
Dysfunctional Communication and Goals in Responses to Stress

Satir's stress positions	Words	Feelings	Self (S), others (O), and social context (C)	Thing most avoided	The price paid	Kfir's personality priorities
Placating	Agreement	Anxiety		Rejection	Loss of identity/ too many people to please	Pleasing
Blaming	Disagreement	Anger/irritation		Meaninglessness	Overworked/ overburdened	Superiority/ significance
Super-reasonable	Rational	Irritation/fear to come out		Humiliation/ embarrassment	Social distance	Control
Irrelevant	Distracting	Confusion		Pain and stress	Low productivity	Comfort

dened, even when stress is low, life is going well, and they are handling what challenges life may bring. When stress increases, however, people who blame and seek significance will try to overwhelm their problems; failing that, they find and assign fault to others: "If it weren't for you, everything would be alright" (Satir, 1988, p. 87).

Super-Reasonable–Control

The super-reasonable person seeks control in his or her life. The head is programmed to take information in, to sort, and to report only that which is deemed clearly rational. Anything else would introduce "messiness" into communication. Feelings are considered prime causes of irrational messiness. The super-reasonable–control person, therefore, tries to turn all feelings off from the neck down (Satir, 1988). Such people seek a life guided by principle within a managed context or situation. This effort to control emotions inevitably leads to a sacrifice of self and others. The communication is rational, abstract, and often long, even when inappropriate: Sounding controlled is at least as important as being in control.

Under stress, super-reasonable people seek to control others or situations in an effort to avoid embarrassment or humiliation. Social distance becomes preferable to emotional contact, and isolation is often the price that is paid. Such a person often seeks activities that can be performed with exactness—and alone.

Irrelevant–Comfort

Comfort has a special meaning in Kfir's typology: Rather than a *seeking* of pleasure and ease, it is an avoidance of stress and pain. In this sense, it is a very narrowly constructed experience of comfort. When stress goes up, people with this priority do anything to distract. The communication tends to become irrelevant: Such people answer a question with a question; they change the subject; or their statements seem to have missing parts, transitions, or connections. Irrelevant communications never quite fit the context or the needs of the situation.

The irrelevant–comfort person knows that disagreements tend to produce distress. The best way to avoid the discomfort of conflict is to simply never take a stand. The problem with irrelevance is that no one pays attention to the person, and the person almost always has trouble focusing on significant problems in life. Their productivity suffers along with their self-worth, because most of us gain a sense of worth through our efforts in meeting the tasks of life.

These four communication stances/priorities comprise a four-by-four typology. As such, they do not tell us everything there is to know about a person. They are, however, a matrix for understanding human action and interaction when people are coping with real or perceived difficulties. Although no one has just one way of communicating, the concept of a priority seems to fit: We all have a first line of defense, a reliable, first preference in safeguarding ourselves. Still, an individual may use any or all of these dysfunctional processes, depending on the people involved and the demands of the situation.

In group counseling, this typology has three very important functions.

1. Through self-reflection, people who are new to group leadership can explore their personal *triggers*, and monitor how they might normally tend to respond under stress.
2. It helps group counselors understand the positions that various group members may take. It replaces what may initially be a critical judgment of a group member with an avenue for understanding the person's coping process.
3. It provides the group counselor or therapist with another means of intervention that will help group members become aware of their interactive process and perhaps make different response choices.

If we return to an interaction between Erv and Dr. Sonstegard from the session in chapter 2, we can examine the effects of a very direct—and yet therapeutic—intervention. In the session, Dr. Sonstegard has just noted that another group member has functioned as a rebel.

Erv: I think most people are rebels.
Sonstegard: Do you feel you are?
Erv: Yeah. I despise anything my mom and dad want me to do. Most of the time I do it to keep from getting in too much trouble, but I do it my way. My way is right, and their way is wrong.
Sonstegard: Because you're so superior?
Erv: Of course.

Here, what initially seems like a rather angry (and blaming) comment also reveals Erv's goal of significance and superiority. When Dr. Sonstegard suggests this to him, even in a direct manner, Erv does not flinch from accepting it. It fits for him. It invites no resistance. He feels understood, and he responds, "Of course."

The other three communication stances–priorities are present in a different group session involving graduate students in a Department of Counseling. The group has just heard one of the members, Tami, talk about her fiancé and his family. Her anxiety is palpable as she reports that the wife of her fiancé's brother has just tried to kill this future brother-in-law in his sleep. Tami's fiancé has talked of going with his older brother to "kill this woman," a prospect Tami finds unlikely, but it still scares her. She keeps saying, "I just want them to all get along. I want to be supportive of my fiancé, but I don't want him to go to jail. I want this all to stop. I feel like I have to fix this. I just want everyone to get along." In the following segment, we revisit a group we have introduced before: Along with Tami, the group members are Angela, Rebecca, Pat, and Chad.

Angela:	I don't get it. Why doesn't his brother just divorce the woman? Why would he choose to stay with someone who tried to kill him? She's just nuts.
Tami:	She's very nuts. But what if James [her fiancé] does go after her? Then, he'll be nuts or worse—in jail. I don't want to hurt his feelings, but ... (waving her arms up and down) I just want everyone to get along.
Rebecca:	You're feeling very scared by all of this. (Tami nods.)
Pat:	I think you should tell him you're scared and that you don't want him to do anything crazy.
Tami:	I don't think I can do that. Maybe I should just go with him anytime he goes up to his brother's house.
Counselor:	Tami, what are you feeling right now?
Tami:	Scared, like she said.
Counselor:	Would you close your eyes for a moment and tell me where you feel this scare in your body? (Tami points to her stomach.) What does it feel like there?
Tami:	A rock. A hard rock.
Counselor:	Does it have a temperature? (Tami shakes her head "no.") Does it have a shape?
Tami:	Hard and smooth.

Counselor: Okay, "hard and smooth." Now, I want you to think back to the earliest time you can remember having this feeling of a hard, smooth rock that is you being scared: What do you remember?

There is a long pause, and then some tears start to roll down Tami's face. The counselor asks Tami what she is remembering. She remembers being about 5 years old and her brother telling her that she is adopted and that she is not really part of the family. It scares her, and even when she finds out she wasn't adopted, she still feels hurt and fears being left behind.

Counselor: Are your tears about this feeling of being hurt?
Tami: Partly. And partly, I just miss my brother.
Counselor: He lives far away from you? (Tami nods.) Do you see how this loss of your brother is all tied up in your fears for your fiancé?
Rebecca: And maybe you feel you have to be so involved in this because you don't want to feel set aside, left out, or rejected again?

Pat moves closer to Tami in the group and puts her hand on Tami's shoulder, offering support. Pat has tears that seem to match Tami's tears. When the counselor asks Angela and Rebecca how they are doing, both express sympathy for Tami. Angela notes that even with tears, Tami seems calmer than she did earlier. When the counselor asks Chad how he is doing, however, he replies: "I don't really have a response to any of this. I know it is important to her, but it really doesn't affect me. I don't know what else to say."

In the responses of group members to Tami, each is clear that a difficult issue is being addressed, and each is struggling to find the right thing to say. Angela's initial response comes from a super reasonable-control position. Tami's situation seems out of control to her, and she wants to assert a logical principle ("just divorce the woman") that she hopes will end the problem and reassert order.

Rebecca's response acknowledges that there are feelings in Tami that need to be addressed. Pat, too, recognizes these feelings, but she is looking to see who has fault for Tami's fears: In her mind, Tami's fiancé owns this problem, and Tami should just tell him not to do anything crazy. Pat has the hope that if her suggestion is taken, she will have preserved a sense of being right and will have provided a meaningful solution (an example of blaming–significance).

The counselor uses an Adlerian approach for easing difficult feelings through early recollections (Janoe & Janoe, 1973, 1979) to help Tami and other group members discover the relationship of Tami's current concerns with some very old fears of rejection and loss. Tami's attempts to placate and please throughout this group segment make sense when we consider the interpretation of life contained in her early memory. Her early recollection is a constant reminder to her that men may dismiss her at any time and she can be left all alone.

Chad's response may actually feed her concern. It can easily be read as another dismissal of her. He seems to be more than just quiet. He is staying actively disengaged. Even when asked to participate, he doesn't want to take a stand. There is almost a declaration that he cannot find in himself a capacity for empathy with Tami. Within our typology, however, his remarks are simply irrelevant. He seeks the comfort of withdrawal, not wanting to even recognize someone else's feelings of hurt or pain.

While all four communication-priority positions are represented in this group counseling segment, human beings are not limited to one or more of these four styles. Some people face the problems of life in a more balanced, functional manner characterized by *congruence* (Satir, Stachowiak, & Taschman, 1975) and *social interest* (Adler, 1938) (see Table 6.2). Rather than turning *stress into distress* (Selye, 1974), they engage others with emotional honesty, preserving a sense of self-worth while also considering the needs of others and of the situation or the context in which people are functioning. They look for win–win solutions and seek to behave in ways that "earn [their] neighbor's love" (Selye, 1974, p. 131). In the preceding segment, Rebecca seems to represent such a position.

Congruence–Social Interest

Congruent people tend to approach stressful situations more holistically, keeping in mind their own needs, the needs of others, and the needs of any given situation. Instead of treating distress as a life block, difficulties are accepted as a normal part of life, a challenge to be met. People in this position are more flexible, consider options, and negotiate differences. What they have to say matches how they feel and what they experience. This emotional honesty is characterized by

Table 6.2
Functional Communication and Goals in Response to Stress

Satir's stress positions	Words	Feelings	Self (S), others (O), and social context (C)	How the person faces stress	Resources	Adler's number 1 priority
Congruence	Words match feelings and experience/use of "I" statements	Calm Balanced/centered	(diagram: circle divided into S, O, C)	Courage/confidence	Personal sense, talents, and connections with others; choices and options	Social interest

integrity. "Anything can be talked about; anything can be commented on; any question can be raised; there is nothing to hold back" (Satir et al., 1975, p. 49). The result is personal accountability, clarity of communication, and a consideration of options and real choices.

Adlerians believe that the social interest that flows from a sense of belonging—from having a community feeling—provides people with the courage and confidence they need to cope well with life (Sweeney, 1998). Such people do not feel alone in the world. They contribute to the well-being of others and allow others to contribute to their lives. In this sense, many of life's problems become group tasks, making use of multiple resources from any number of people who might be involved. Group counseling and group therapy are perfect settings for the nurturance of this community feeling. The group process requires that we lend a hand when we can. It also allows us to ask for help with clarity when we need it. And both transactions can be accomplished without any group member feeling diminished.

OBSERVATION OF GROUP PROCESS OVER AN EXTENDED PERIOD OF TIME

Toward the beginning of this book, we detailed a single group session with adolescents that we hoped would be illustrative of initial group process. A single session, however, is no substitute for experiencing and observing group process over an extended period of time. Indeed, even experiencing and observing often need to be separate acts. It is hard to both be "in" an experience and observe it at the same time. When possible, we like counselors and therapists to have a group experience that is at least a semester long (about 15 to 16 weeks). We would also like these future group leaders to have an equal amount of time—often concurrently with the group experience—to observe at least two ongoing groups with participants of different age levels and in two different settings.

Journaling and Electronic Communication

We feel that nothing supports observations quite as well as a journaling process where observers are able to note what they see and hear as well as what meaning the observed experience has for them. For years, we encouraged our students to use a split-half method of journaling similar to the way in which the group session was presented in chapter 2 of this book. On the left side of a page or on the left half of two pages that face each other in a journal, we asked group leaders-in-training to note as accurately as possible what happened in the group session. On the right side, we would then want them to comment on what they had noticed: to consider what meaning it had for them and what they were learning; to consider what they would feel like as a group member or the group leader; and to speculate about what they might have done differently and why.

Such journals often resulted in small books documenting the student's learning and development. The writing in these journals often became increasingly personal as observers grew more comfortable with reflective practice and the issues generated in groups touched real issues in the observers' lives. These journals were a way for both the group leader-in-training and a supervisor to create a focus for professional development of the counselor or therapist. The difficulties in reviewing observational journals were that we interrupted the journaling process for observers when we had their journals, we tended to feel overwhelmed by the sheer volume of reading required, and we were often weeks behind in providing encouragement and feedback. This was especially true when many observers were watching many different groups.

With the advent of electronic learning systems, the use of web-based programs has made this observational process infinitely more manageable. Although there are many different electronic learning systems from which to choose, we use and are most familiar with *Blackboard* (Blackboard, Inc., 2003). This system allows us to manage a number of observation and reporting processes simultaneously, with the specific advantage of allowing student-observers to see the same group sessions over many weeks, record their reflections in electronic journals, and receive almost immediate feedback.

For example, we have used Blackboard's group designation process to form small groups of observers that will all see the same sessions in a location close to where they live. Each member of these Blackboard groups has access to a computer-based discussion board, a virtual classroom (or chat room), e-mail messaging, and a digital drop box. The discussion board allows the observational group members to pose questions to each other, to seek clarification about group process or what was observed, and to share individual perspectives on the experience. This process can happen over an extended period of time, so that people can check in and out of the system at their convenience. The virtual classroom is more immediate: It requires that all parties log onto the chat room at the same time. It allows the observers to discuss issues, content, and process as if they were all present in the same room. Both discussion boards and virtual classroom interactions are archived, allowing Blackboard group members and their supervisor to review what is being discussed and what is being learned at a later time.

The e-mail function provides a more direct means of communication and can be accessed from Blackboard's e-mail address book for all participants. This function tends to be used when individual members are arranging time together or when they wish to communicate directly with the supervisor.

The digital drop box serves as a holding place for submitted work. Observers can use any word processing program (e.g., *Microsoft Word*) to journal and reflect upon their observations. Then, by using Blackboard's digital drop box, they can post their journal for the supervisor. The supervisor, in turn, can use the "comment" function available in most word-processing programs to respond to the submitted journals—or the supervisor can simply write a response as another entry in the journal itself. The response is then sent electronically back to the observer's digital drop box. No paper has been used. No hard-copy journals have been exchanged.

Because observers tend to submit their digital journals over a number of days (rather than at the same time), the ability of the supervisor to handle the volume is greatly increased. There is also the option of allowing journal reflections to be shared with other group observers. And most importantly, we can ask the group leader(s) to also journal from their more experienced position(s) about the group process and post these reflections for all observers to consider.

Learning About Groups and Accessing Supervisor Responses

Over time, groups change in both character and process. A number of group texts have suggested that groups progress through identifiable stages—each with different tasks and functions (Corey, 2000; Corey & Corey, 2002; Gladding, 2003; Yalom, 1995). Kottler (2001) lists a range of stages from two to five associated with different models—with three to four stages being the most common. Stages of groups, however, serve mainly as a process-construct for leaders, an aid in helping the group counselor or therapist to track the actions and interactions of group members.

In general, we expect the early sessions of group counseling or therapy to address issues of safety and trust, in addition to whatever other idiosyncratic issues might emerge given the composition of the group. During the early sessions, we expect that the group leader will take a more active role in the group, modeling effective listening and inquiry skills while also providing structures for understanding self and others. We have already noted in earlier chapters the importance of a democratic atmosphere, mutual respect, and reflective communication in encouraging group participation and the development of individual voices within the group.

> Treatment itself is an exercise in cooperation and a test of cooperation. We succeed only if we are genuinely interested in the other. We must be able to see with his eyes and hear with his ears. He must contribute his part to our common understanding. We must work out his attitudes and his difficulties together. Even if we felt we had understood him, we should have no witness that we were right unless he also understood. A tactless truth can never be the whole truth; it shows that our understanding was not sufficient. (Adler, 1931, p. 72)

It is in the middle segments of group process that psychological investigations can lead to a better understanding of self and others. Although there are many interventions that contribute to this process, we have focused throughout the book on those investigative avenues that are distinctly Adlerian: an investigation within group process of birth order and family constellation; a consideration of member approaches to the life tasks; and an understanding of the meaning of early memories or early recollections. These three avenues are recursive; that is, the coping stances one takes in relation to birth order, the tasks of life, and early experiences all affect one another, creating a kind of unity of style in the process of change. Any or all of these avenues help a group leader to understand and anticipate what process and movement each member will bring to the group experience. They also provide practitioners and students alike with a process for seeking meaningful supervision with clients. Professional colleagues who are experienced in lifestyle assessments have always been willing to share their thoughts and perspective on the more objective aspects of lifestyle data, and this collaboration—even through e-mail—has often opened up new possibilities for working with clients.

A psychological understanding of self and others provides a foundation for working on current issues and goals that group members bring to group process. Sometimes a new knowledge of self is experienced as insight, but insight is just one form of awareness. The goal in group is to achieve a more public integration of awareness and meaning that leads to a real knowing of self by others, a real understanding of one's place and value in the group. Such understanding is a replacement for the critical judgment of others and produces both empathy and caring in most people.

Although we do not focus on cohesion as an intended group outcome, we recognize that such bonding often occurs as people participate in personal work with each other. We also believe that the real work of groups happens between members rather than between the group leader and the members. As groups become more effective in empathic responding, support, problem solving, redirection, and reorientation, an effective group leader intervenes less. In many cases, the leader's role may start to blend with the role of participants, and self-disclosures on the part of the counselor or therapist may increase.

Our guidelines for self-disclosure always start with the question of purpose: What purpose will a self-disclosure serve in the group process? The most valued self-disclosures have the purposes of (a) normalizing experiences for group members, (b) modeling support and connection through a sharing of personal responses, and (c) providing indirect learning through a consideration of what has been useful in the therapist's life and experience. Each of these goals for self-disclosure reflects the mandate to keep the needs of individuals and the group at the forefront of any intervention. This being said, such personal interventions by the group leader tend to increase as the group begins to function more autonomously—especially toward the end of group when reaching closure becomes a central task.

We believe that there are two times when groups may need more structure. In time-limited, closed groups, these times are at the very beginning of the group sessions and, again, at the end. In the beginning, structure provides a sense of security and safety-through-agreements that are essential for group development. Toward the end of groups, it becomes increasingly clear that the experience will stop: that this place where people have come to share their lives will not be available anymore. Although we sometimes mitigate the experience of loss by agreeing to additional meetings 6 months or a year later, a scheduled form of brief intermittent therapy (Bitter & Nicoll, 2000), this is not always possible.

We meet people in the middle of their lives, and, for the most part, we leave them in the middle of their lives. Loss, and the sadness that often accompanies it, is always a part of endings. In groups, participants often seem almost in grief over the ending of a positive group experience. And in such cases, group members may become unusually quiet, not wanting to get into anything that cannot be completed and wondering how to say what matters most to them.

When we know that the amount of time to achieve closure is limited, we will ask group members to repeat a process that we often use at the beginning of a group. We will ask them, once again, to pair off and to interview a partner about the following topics: (a) what experience has meant the most to them in the group; (b) what personal goals were present in the group and what progress did each person make; (c) what did participants learn about self and others, and how will these new understandings be used in the rest of their lives; and (d) what things went unsaid that someone may still feel a need to say.

We also ask group members to consider how they handle loss and how they choose to say "goodbye" when it means something. Any kind of change involves loss—even though many personal changes may be described as natural or as developmental transitions. A young woman achieves adulthood with the start of her menstrual cycle, but she also loses her childhood. Secondary school ends, and young people go off to college or the world of work, perhaps leaving behind the safety of family. A couple chooses to have children, and they lose some of their exclusive intimacy in the choice to begin a family. In any change, there is always something lost and something gained, a little grief even within the relief or celebration of new possibilities. Even when people choose not to change, they lose what might have been. Again, birth order and early recollections often anticipate how people will cope. When early memories of loss or death are vividly present in certain members, linking these early experiences to the group's ending process can often help people complete both the group and unfinished experiences from the past.

GROUP THEORY, COLEADERSHIP, AND SUPERVISION

Group experience and group observations provide the foundation for understanding and integrating group theory. Too often, professional training programs start with courses on group theory and/or group process before either the class or its literature can have much relevance. We want theory and practice to relate to real experience and to provide an opportunity for reflection upon the real events people have observed or in which they have participated.

For this reason, a course on group process might be designed in such a way that experience, guidance, coleadership, and theoretical foundations are all integrated. In a 3-hour course, 10 to 16 group members can also be divided into coleadership teams. Using either Blackboard (Blackboard, Inc., 2003) tools or meeting face-to-face outside of class, these five to eight coleadership teams can discuss and plan their group leadership process based on (a) what they have both experienced and observed, (b) consultation with the course instructor/ supervisor, and (c) readings related to group process and practice.

From the very beginning of the course, we would want the first 2 hours of class devoted to a group experience. Over 16 weeks, the people in the course would be members of a group process, and each team would then have a minimum of two 2-hour group sessions to conduct. The group experience would be followed by a final hour of "debriefing" or process consultation in which the course instructor would facilitate feedback for the coleaders and a consideration of group theory, the roles of the group leaders, effective intervention skills, and the actual group process. Although the course instructor would be available if the coleaders felt they needed immediate guidance, coleaders would be encouraged to go as far as they could with the group process.

As an alternative to students being both group members and group leaders, we also believe that the first 2 hours can involve work with people from outside of the class. This is especially useful when training counselors who will one day work with children or adolescents. We still hold—under these circumstances—to live, hands-on work with the coleadership of the group rotating through the class. In such sessions, the coleaders often work in an inner circle with the rest of the class members observing the group from a second, larger, outside and concentric circle. Because we want every course member involved in the process, we have adapted Tom Andersen's (1991) model of reflecting teams to group training.

With about 30 to 40 minutes left in the group process, we ask the people in the two circles to switch places with the group members and their leaders in the outer circle and the observers in the inner circle. We ask the observers to reflect honestly and caringly to what they have seen and heard. These reflections often elicit metaphors and reframings that are useful to group members and the group process as a whole. We ask: What is it that—if added to the group—would facilitate the growth of one or more group members or help the group process develop? What has been noticed that seemed significant and useful? What impressions have the group members left with those observing? The focus is always on encouragement. A reflecting team is generally not a good place for criticism, disagreements with leadership or process, or demonstrations of outside competence. We want each member of the reflecting team to bring something real from within themselves to the group, keeping in mind the people who will receive the shared information, and communicating with tact and timing.

With about 10 to 15 minutes left in the group process, we ask the group members and the reflecting team to again switch places. The coleaders help the original group members process what they have heard from the reflecting team. At the end of a session, a summary of what has happened and what meanings have been introduced to the process generally sets the stage for the next group meeting. This live experience and feedback process has proved no more cumbersome in group training than it did in family therapy. The benefits for both the rotating group leaders and the group members multiply as the input from a diversity of sources is received.

It is our experience that both coleadership processes and supervision of group leaders in practicum and internship settings suffer the most from supervisor criticism. We all began our professions with less skills than we have learned over the years. Young practitioners need plenty of room to make mistakes as well as achieve creative wonders. Focusing on what has gone well and the qualities of the leadership that are effective is the foundation for good supervision. Adlerians believe that all people grow from the courage that comes with success, from a consideration of personal strengths, and from confidence gained in experience.

We often start our group supervision courses with a discussion of the fears and concerns counselors- and therapists-in-training might have. It is in the sharing of mutual worries that the burden diminishes. We also reassure our trainees that we are all in this process together. When we go to a school or community agency to conduct supervision, we, as supervisors, are present in the group. We listen, we learn, we consult when asked to do so, and, most importantly, we initiate post-group discussions about leadership and process based on encouragement. Questions that initiate reflection in trainees are far more useful that direct advice.

As supervisors, when we are asked to help out, we want to do so in a manner that facilitates movement while leaving the leadership of the therapist-in-training intact. In his early nineties, Dr. Sonstegard is still providing group supervision in England. One of the groups with which he worked included five teenagers, two girls and three boys. These teenagers were all young people no longer in school, but who voluntarily came every day to a halfway house. They spent the day from 8:00 a.m. to 5:00 p.m. in the care of social workers. In addition to educational activities, these young people cooked their own meals and kept the house clean.

Millie was a student of social work who had counseled the group for two or three sessions. The three boys had been difficult during each of the sessions. The two girls, Jill and Lois, were interested and congenial participants. Jill was about 14 years old, but looked 18. She was well developed for a girl her age. Lois was smaller, slim, and had yet to develop. Jill and Lois usually sat together to the left of the social worker in the circle. The boys sat on the right side of the circle.

When Dr. Sonstegard joined the group, however, Lois sat between Millie, the social worker, and Dr. Sonstegard. Jill kept motioning to Lois, trying to entice her to sit beside her, as she always had done. But Lois did not move. It was as if she wanted protection—perhaps from the boy's teasing: protection that she did not feel she could get any longer sitting next to Jill.

Millie started the group session by introducing Dr. Sonstegard as her supervisor and asking if it would be okay for him to sit in. With this agreement, she asked what the group would like to discuss, but nothing was forthcoming. Mostly, the boys whispered and giggled, glancing at Jill, turning to each other, and then whispering and giggling some more. Millie asked the group what they felt was going on, but again, no one had much to say.

Dr. Sonstegard asked Millie, "Do you need any help?"

She answered, "I really feel like I am in trouble here. Anything you can do would be greatly appreciated."

Dr. Sonstegard turned to the group and said, "Millie asked a very good question when she wondered what was going on. And I think I know. Would you like to know what I think?"

Even though no one answered, all of the group members were looking at Dr. Sonstegard. He looked at Jill, but said to the boys, "She is built pretty good, isn't she?" All the whispering and giggling stopped, and the boys sat back in their chairs, wanting to disappear. Dr. Sonstegard continued, "I think Harry likes you, Jill." Jill smiled and smoothed her dress. "And the other boys are trying to prove to Harry that they like you too," he continued.

Now, Dr. Sonstegard turned to Millie. "What do you think about what I have said to them?" The boys were now slumped in their chairs, trying to make themselves invisible. Millie turned back to Jill and asked her what it was like to have all this attention directed at her. Jill noted that she liked it, but that she did not want to lose Lois as a friend. She also wished the boys were more considerate. Dr. Sonstegard returned to listening, and Millie blended nicely back into her role as group leader.

Dr. Sonstegard's intervention is one that is perhaps easier to make when the supervisor is older and has gained a certain amount of wisdom. It was designed to bring out into the open what was happening behind the scenes, not just in the group, but throughout the house. It was also designed to redirect a competent social worker without taking over.

Some weeks later, when Dr. Sonstegard was invited to the "house" for tea, the coordinator of the social service inquired about the group's sessions. He was interested, he said, because the disturbances caused by the boys' teasing and hassling of the girls had stopped.

Summary

In this chapter, we have proposed a group training program that we believe would be effective with any model of group counseling or therapy. It is our hope that the education of group counselors and therapists will have at least as much emphasis as those who train in individual counseling and therapy receive. In the best of all situations, we would like to see group leaders receive the same sort of hands-on experience and guidance that medical students receive in their specialties. Our ideal would include: a group experience for all people entering the professions of counseling, social work, or psychology; observation of group process over an extended period of time; didactic training in group theory, group process, and group evaluation directly related to personal group experiences and observed processes; coleadership of groups under supervision; and finally, a practicum or internship with a prominent use of group work and adequate supervision.

In an effort to facilitate this model, we have used a combination of Satir's (1976) communication stances and Kfir's (1971, 1989; Kfir & Corsini, 1981) personality priorities as a means of helping group counselors-in-training learn about personal triggers and have a mechanism for making initial observations and assessments of group process. We also noted our use of journaling and electronic media as a means of reflective practice and communication between students and between students and supervisors. Finally, we revisited the larger flow of group counseling and therapy as it pertains to training, education, and processes for supervision.

REFERENCES

Adler, A. (1931). *What life should mean to you*. New York: Grosset & Dunlap.
Adler, A. (1938). *Social interest: The challenge to mankind*. London: Faber & Faber.
Andersen, T. (1991). *The reflecting team: Dialogues and dialogues about the dialogues*. New York: Norton.
Ansbacher, H. L. (1992). Alfred Adler's concept of community feeling and of social interest and the relevance of community feeling for old age. *Individual Psychology, 48*(4), 402–412.
Bitter, J. R. (1987). Communication and meaning: Satir in Adlerian context. In R. Sherman & D. Dinkmeyer (Eds.), *Systems of family therapy: An Adlerian integration* (pp. 109–142). New York: Brunner/Mazel.
Bitter, J. R. (1993). Communication styles, personality priorities, and social interest: Strategies for helping couples build a life together. *Individual Psychology, 49*(3/4), 330–350.
Bitter, J. R., & Nicoll, W. G. (2000). Adlerian brief therapy with individuals: Process and practice. *Journal of Individual Psychology, 56*(1), 31–44.
Blackboard, Inc. (2003). About Blackboard. Retrieved 24 April, 2003, from http://www.blackboard.com/about/index.htm.
Corey, G. (2000). *Theory and practice of group counseling* (5th ed.). Pacific Grove, CA: Brooks-Cole/Wadsworth.
Corey, M. S., & Corey, G. (2002). *Groups: Process and practice* (6th ed.). Pacific Grove, CA: Brooks-Cole/Wadsworth.
Gilligan, C. (1982). *In a different voice*. Cambridge, MA: Harvard University Press.
Gladding, S. T. (2003). *Group work: A counseling specialty* (4th ed.). Upper Saddle River, NJ: Merrill/Prentice Hall.
Janoe, E., & Janoe, B. (1973). *Dealing with feelings*. Vancouver, WA: Family Life Enrichment Center.
Janoe, E., & Janoe, B. (1979). Dealing with feelings via early recollections. In H. A. Olson (Ed.), *Early recollections: Their use in diagnosis and psychotherapy* (pp. 206–222). Springfield, IL: Charles C Thomas.
Kfir, N. (1971, July). *Priorities: A different approach to life style and neurosis*. Paper presented at ICASSI, Tel Aviv, Israel.
Kfir, N. (1989). *Crisis intervention verbatim*. New York: Hemisphere.
Kfir, N., & Corsini, R. J. (1981). Impasse/priority therapy. In R. J. Corsini (Ed.), *Handbook of innovative psychotherapies* (pp. 401–415). New York: Wiley.
Kottler, J. A. (2001). *Learning group leadership: An experiential approach*. Boston: Allyn & Bacon.

Pelonis, P. (2002). *Facing change in the journey of life*. Athens, Greece: Fytraki Publications.

Powers, R. L., & Griffith, J. (1987). *Understanding lifestyle: The psycho-clarity process*. Chicago: AIAS.

Rapin, L., & Keel, L. (1998). Association for specialists in group work best practice guidelines. *Journal for Specialists in Group Work, 23*(3), 237–244.

Satir, V. (1976). *Making contact*. Millbrae, CA: Celestial Arts.

Satir, V. (1988). *The new peoplemaking*. Palo Alto, CA: Science and Behavior Books.

Satir, V., Stachowiak, J., & Taschman, H. A. (1975). *Helping families to change*. New York: Jason Aronson.

Selye, H. (1974). *Stress without distress*. New York: Signet.

Sweeney, T. J. (1998). *Adlerian counseling: A practitioner's approach* (4th ed.). Philadelphia, PA: Accelerated Development.

Yalom, I. D. (1995). *The theory and practice of group psychotherapy* (4th ed.). New York: Basic Books.

Authors' Notes

Manford A. Sonstegard, PhD, is Professor Emeritus at the Marshall University Graduate College in Charleston, WV. He currently lives in Stow-on-the-Wold, England, with his wife Rita. He is the current president of the Adlerian Society of the United Kingdom and the Institute for Individual Psychology. He is also a past president of the North American Society of Adlerian Psychology (NASAP). In addition to his many articles, chapters, and booklets, he has offered training on four continents and established Adlerian family education centers in many countries.

James Robert Bitter, EdD, is professor of counseling at the East Tennessee State University in Johnson City, TN. He lives with his wife and partner, Lynn Williams, and their two daughters, Alison and Nora Williams. He is a diplomate in Adlerian Psychology (NASAP) and has served on the Delegate Assembly of that organization. He has also been the editor of the *Journal of Individual Psychology*. He is a founding faculty member of the Adlerian Training Institute in Boca Raton, FL, and he is known for his work in developing Adlerian Brief Therapy.

Peggy Pelonis, MA, is professor of counseling at the University of LaVerne in Athens, Greece. She lives with her husband, Bill Peneros, and her daughter, Lydia. She has been the president of the Greek Adlerian Society, and she conducts a private practice in Athens. She has written a book, *Facing Change in the Journey of Life* (2002) that is based on her many years of experience and training in the Human Validation Process Model of Virginia Satir.

Indexes

Name Index

A

Adler, A., *ix–x, xviii–xix, xx*, 4, 6–7, 14, 16, 47, 55, 60, 62, 63, 70, 71, 73, 74, 77, 78, 80, 81, 90–91, 95, 96–97, 98–99, 118, 121, 126–128, 130, 134, 139, 157, 171, 172, 176, 183
Albert, L., 13, 14, 137, 141, 157
Andersen, T., 102, 130, 179, 183
Ansbacher, H. L., 61, 62, 80, 86, 90, 91, 96, 99, 110, 118, 121, 130–131, 132, 134, 145, 157, 163, 183
Ansbacher, R. R., 61, 80, 86, 90, 91, 96, 99, 110, 118, 121, 130–131, 132, 134
Aristotle, 6, 126, 131
Atkins, E. M., 131
Austin, K. M., 126, 131

B

Baird, K. L., 153, 159
Bardige, B., 9, 15
Baruth, L., 71, 91, 153, 158
Belenky, M. F., 101, 132
Bellah, R. N., 126, 131
Benton, W., 73, 92
Bitter, J. R., *ix, x, xv, xvii, xix, xx, xxi*, 12, 15, 18, 56, 60, 64, 70, 74, 78, 86, 89, 91, 92, 97, 103, 112, 114, 117, 127, 131, 133, 146, 148, 151, 153, 154, 157, 159, 160, 161, 164, 177, 183
Bronowski, J., 96, 131

C

Callanan, P., 112, 126, 131
Carlson, J., 13, 14, 70, 91, 106, 131, 137, 141, 158
Christensen, O. C., 13, 14, 60, 91, 96, 102, 114, 131, 141, 157
Cicero, M. T., 126, 131
Clark, A., 44, 56, 81, 82, 91
Clinchy, B. M., 101, 132
Copleston, F., 6, 14, 97, 131
Corey, G., 11, 12, 14, 100, 112, 117, 123, 125, 126, 131, 136, 157, 175, 183
Corey, M. S., 12, 14, 100, 112, 117, 123, 125, 126, 131, 136, 157, 175, 183
Corsini, R. J., *xx*, 56, 60, 88, 91, 96, 97, 131, 132, 133, 141, 158, 161, 163, 182, 183

D

Darwin, C., 4, 14
DeOrnellas, K., 153, 158
Dinkmeyer, D., *xx*, 13, 14, 56, 109, 114, 131, 137, 141, 158, 183
Dinkmeyer, J. S., 137, 141, 158
Dinkmeyer, Jr., D., 13, 14, 70, 91, 106, 131, 137, 141, 158
Dreikurs, R., *ix, x, xv, xvi, xviii, xx, xxi*, 4, 5, 7, 8, 12, 15, 18, 41, 42, 52, 56, 60, 62, 70, 78, 79, 80, 85, 91, 92, 96, 97, 98, 99, 101, 102, 103, 105, 106, 109, 112, 121, 124, 127, 131, 132, 133, 135, 136, 137, 138, 140, 141–145, 146, 148, 151, 153, 154, 155, 157, 158, 159
Dushman, R. D., 153, 158

E

Eckstein, D., 71, 91, 153, 158, 159
Epston, D., 7, 15

189

F

Feit, S., *xv*
Foucault, M., 7, 15
Frankl, V., *ix*
Freeman, S. L., 15
Freud, S., 6, 15, 6, 132, 134
Furtmuller, C., 127–128, 132, 134

G

Gay, P., 132
Gazda, G. M., *xx*, *xxi*, 15, 56, 97, 125, 128, 132, 133, 136, 151, 158, 159
Gergen, K., 7, 15
Gilligan, C., 9, 15, 101, 124, 132, 163, 183
Gladding, S. T., 163, 175, 183
Glasser, W., 139, 158
Glueck, B., 130
Goldberger, N. R., 101, 132
Gottman, J., 96, 132, 137, 158, 159
Griffith, J., 71, 78, 92, 153, 159, 163, 184
Griffin, M. T., 131
Grunwald, B. B., 74, 91, 137, 141, 158, 159

H

Hart, B., 96, 100, 132, 136, 159
Hawes, C., 60, 91
Henderson, V. L., 118, 121, 133
Hoffman, E., 6, 15, 60, 91, 98, 132, 139, 159
Hooven, C., 137, 159

I

Irwin, T., 131

J

Janoe, B., 171, 183
Janoe, E., 171, 183
Jensen, E., 157
Jensen, F., 157

K

Katz, L. F., 137, 159

Keel, L., 163, 184
Kern, R. M., 153, 159
Kfir, N., 23, 50, 56, 102, 132, 161, 163, 164–168, 182, 183
Kirschenbaum, H., 118, 121, 133
Kjos, D., 91, 157
Krestensen, K. K., 114, 133
Kottler, J. A., 175, 183
Kottman, T., 153, 158, 159

L

Lewis, J. A., 13, 14
Lieberman, M. A., 128, 133
Lind, J. E., 130
Linton, J., 130
Lisiecki, J., 117, 133
Lowe, R. N., 96, 132, 141, 145, 154, 158, 159

M

Madsen, R., 126, 131
Manaster, G., 96, 133
Maslow, A., *ix*, 98, 133
May, R., *ix*
McAbee, H., 74, 91, 141, 159
McGoldrick, M., 73, 92
McKay, G., 13, 14, 114, 131, 137, 141, 158
McKay, J., 137, 141, 158
McNamee, S., 7, 15
Miles, M. B., 128, 133
Millican, V., 153, 158
Moline, M. E., 126, 131
Mosak, H. H., *xix*, *xx*, 62, 71, 78, 79, 81, 91, 92, 153, 159
Mozdzierz, G. J., 117, 133
Muro, J. J., 15

N

Nicoll, W. G., 60, 89, 91, 92, 177, 183

O

Ohlsen, M. M., *xx*, 112, 133, 159
Olson, H. A., 44, 56

Name Index

P

Pelonis (Peneros), P., *xvii, xx*, 60, 62, 79, 92, 161, 164, 184
Pepper, F. C., 137, 141, 158
Pew, W. L., 60, 92, 96, 133
Phillips, A. S., 74, 92
Phillips, C. R., 74, 92
Polster, E., 10, 15, 92, 98, 105, 133
Polster, M., 10, 15, 90, 92, 105, 133
Popkin, M., 13, 15, 114, 133, 137, 141, 159
Porter, A., 130
Powers, R. L., 71, 78, 92, 153, 159, 163, 184

R

Radin, P., 130
Rapin. L., 163, 184
Ratay, J. J., 96, 133
Risley, T. R., 96, 100, 132, 136, 159
Roberts, A., 74, 91, 148, 157
Rogers, C. R., 118, 121, 133

S

Satir, V. M., 64, 92, 114, 115, 117, 118, 133, 161, 163, 164–168, 171–173, 182, 183, 184
Schoenaker, T., 102, 114, 133
Schoenaker, T., 102, 114, 133
Selye, H., 79, 92, 171, 184
Sherman, R., 183
Shifron, R., 62, 92
Shulman, B. H., 71, 92, 153, 159
Soltz, V., 103, 132, 141, 143, 158
Sonnenshein-Schneider, M., 153, 159
Sonstegard, M. A., *ix, x, xv–xxi*, 5, 12, 15, 17, 18, 19–54, 56, 60, 72, 74, 91, 92, 96, 97, 100, 112, 132, 133, 134, 141, 148, 151, 155, 157, 158, 159, 160, 161, 168, 169, 181–182

Sperry, L., 13, 14
Stachowiak, J., 171, 184
Stein. M. I., 91
Sullivan, W. M., 126, 131
Sutherland, J., 153, 158
Sweeney, T., 79, 92, 96, 133, 173, 184
Swindler, A., 126, 131

T

Tarule, J. M., 101, 132
Taschman, H. A., 171, 184
Taylor, J. M., 9, 15
Terner, J., 60, 92, 96, 133
Thoreau, H. D., 8, 15
Tipton, S. M., 126, 131

V

Vaihinger, H., 96, 133
Vaughan, R., 130

W

Walker, E., 151, 159
Ward, J. V., 9, 15
Waterman, J., 151, 159
Watson, M., 73, 92
Wattenburg, W., 112, 133
West, J. D., 86, 91, 127, 131
Wedding, D., *xx*
White, M., 7, 15, 63, 92
Williams, A. L., 117, 133
Williams, G. T., 126, 131
Wolfe, W. B., 14, 55, 90, 130
Wolman, B. B., 158

Y

Yalom, I. D., 12, 15, 64, 92, 100, 112, 113, 114, 116, 117, 125, 128, 133, 134, 136, 159, 175, 184

Subject Index

A

acceptance, 9, 12, 86, 95, 108, 121–122, 129, 130, 149, 152, 155,
Active Parenting, 13, 15, 110, 114, 133, 159
Active Teaching, 159
adaptability, 4, 95, 122–123, 130
Adlerian brief therapy, 55, 60, 62, 89, 91, 92, 177, 183
Adlerian collective therapy, 60
Adlerian counseling, *ix–xi, xv, xvi, xviii, xix–xxi,* 3, 6–14, 15, 17–56, 59, 60, 62, 64, 66–67, 71–72, 75, 76, 80, 81, 84–85, 86–88, 89–90, 95, 96, 102–103, 104, 108, 110, 113, 121, 128, 129, 130, 135–160, 163, 184
Adlerian psychology, *xv, xviii,* 18, 62, 96, 132, 158
Adlerian therapy, *ix, x, xv, xix, xx, xxi,* 3, 6, 8, 10, 12, 13, 14, 59, 60, 62, 64, 75–77, 80, 89, 90, 95, 97–98, 101, 103, 108, 110, 112, 113, 114, 128, 163, 173, 176
adolescence, *xv, xvi, xix, xx,* 5, 7, 13, 15, 18, 20, 35, 46, 55, 65, 66, 68, 97, 103, 105, 108, 111, 113, 114, 117, 119, 121, 122, 138, 141, 152, 153, 155, 156, 173, 179
agreements, group, 19, 23, 26, 55, 59, 61, 66–67, 89, 117, 125–126, 151–152, 177
American Counseling Association (ACA), 55, 91, 129, 130, 159, 162
  ethical code, 19, 55, 64
American Psychiatric Association (APA), 138, 157
American Psychological Association (APA), 162
assertiveness, 9, 95, 104, 119, 130

assessment, *x,* 60, 63, 71, 73, 77, 78, 79, 81, 82, 84, 91, 92, 100, 102–104, 105, 106, 122, 153, 158, 159, 176, 182,
  lifestyle, *x, xviii,* 71, 82, 91, 92, 97, 99, 102, 128, 138, 153, 158, 159, 163, 176, 184
Association of Specialists in Group Work (ASGW), 19, 56, 63, 91, 129, 131
assumed disability, 103, 141, 144, 145, 154
attention deficit disorder (ADD), 139
attention deficit hyperactivity disorder (ADHD), 139
attention getting, 33, 72, 103, 114, 141, 142–143, 144, 145, 147, 148, 149, 154
attitudes, *x,* 98, 176
autocracy, 5, 136
avoidance, 6, 19, 23, 30, 33, 41, 43, 70, 103, 144, 145, 146, 147, 154, 165, 166, 167
awareness, *x,* 7, 43, 45, 47, 70, 98, 99, 100, 101, 105–108, 140, 155, 168, 177

B

beliefs, *x, xi, xviii,* 10, 52, 104, 148
belonging (need to belong), *xix,* 4, 5, 7, 8, 33, 50, 62, 63, 78, 79, 80, 86, 98, 99, 109, 127, 138, 140, 173
birth order, 32, 34, 68, 73, 74, 76, 92, 96, 102, 153, 176, 178
Blackboard, 174, 175, 179, 183
blaming, 164, 165–167, 169, 171
brief therapy, 55, 60, 62, 89, 91, 92, 177, 183

C

CACREP, 162
caring, 80, 90, 95, 121–122, 130, 177, 179

193

Case of Mrs. A., 63, 90
change, 5, 8, 10, 12, 18, 31, 36, 41, 49, 50, 53, 54, 55, 78, 82, 84, 88, 89, 97, 98, 99, 100, 105, 108, 109, 138, 140, 175, 178
  process of, 45, 60, 90, 120, 129, 144, 155, 164, 176, 184
  task of life, 62, 79, 92
child guidance clinics, 6, 16, 60, 96
cognitions, *ix*, 98
cognitive–behavioral, *ix*, 155
collective therapy, 60
comfort, 164, 166, 167–168, 171
community, *xvi, xvii, xix*, 4, 6, 10, 12, 13, 14, 45, 60, 61, 64, 74, 77, 79, 86, 97, 109, 110, 111, 115, 116, 136, 162, 180
community feeling, *x, xviii, xix*, 7, 62, 80, 86, 91, 95, 99, 101, 118, 126, 130, 163, 173, 183
completion, *xviii*, 89, 96, 99, 123, 134, 140
confidence, *xvi, xix*, 7, 26, 31, 46, 62, 79, 80, 86, 95, 110, 119, 122, 127, 130, 156, 172, 173, 180
confidentiality, 25, 26, 67, 126
congruence, *xix*, 172–173
conscious, *xviii*, 84, 98, 99, 103, 131, 135, 140, 145–147, 154, 157
consultation, *xvi, xvii*, 13, 14, 91, 112, 131, 137, 139, 141, 149, 158, 179
control, 164, 166, 167, 170
Cooperative Discipline, 14, 157
"could it be . . . ", 55, 70, 85, 108, 128, 145, 150, 154
counseling children in groups, 136–160
courage, *xix*, 62, 79, 80, 86, 95, 119–121, 122, 126, 130, 172, 173, 180
Creative arts, 153, 158

D

database, 6, 61, 63–64, 73, 176
democracy, *x*, 3, 5–8, 11, 12, 13, 14, 18, 19, 20, 97, 100, 101, 112, 113, 121, 124, 125, 136, 176,
demonstration of adequacy, 148, 149
demonstration of inadequacy, 141, 143, 144, 147, 148, 149
development of voice, 3, 9, 10, 14, 15, 18, 51, 55, 65–66, 101, 113, 132, 136, 163, 176, 183

disclosure(s), 41, 42, 45, 54, 55, 84, 101, 103, 106, 107, 108, 116, 120, 126, 140, 145, 155, 163
  process, 41, 42, 55, 70, 85, 108, 128, 145, 150, 154
  psychological, 6, 12, 18, 41–47, 54, 55, 59, 60, 61, 84–86, 89, 100, 104–108, 121, 128, 157
  self, 128, 177
  tentative, 12, 73, 85, 107, 120, 145, 151, 128,154
discouragement, 7, 53, 78, 97, 99, 109, 119, 122, 141, 143, 149, 150, 152, 164
drawings, 153
dream work, 153
dynamics, *ix*, 56, 62, 63, 97, 120, 132, 136, 155, 158

E

early memories/early recollections, *x*, 44, 56, 59, 61, 68, 71, 80–84, 90, 91, 92, 102, 153, 159, 171, 176, 178, 183
education, *xiii, xv, xx*, 5, 6, 8, 13, 60, 96, 100, 110–111, 114, 128, 132, 136, 139, 141, 157, 161, 162–163, 173–182
electronic media, 161, 173–175, 182
emotions, *ix*, 8, 36, 69, 78, 98, 123, 137, 139, 159, 163, 164, 167, 171
encouragement, *x*, 9, 12, 14, 22, 27, 59, 61, 70, 77, 88, 90, 105, 109, 110, 114, 115, 128, 131, 137, 144, 155, 173, 174, 179, 180
ethical codes, 55, 56, 91, 129, 130, 131
ethics, 81, 95, 126–128, 130, 131
existentialism, *ix x*
existential task, 62, 78, 79
experiential learning, *xix*, 3, 8–9, 10, 14

F

family constellation, *xviii*, 32, 33, 34, 59, 61, 63, 68, 71, 73–77, 90, 93, 102, 142, 152, 153, 176
family education/family counseling, open forum, *xv, xix*, 13, 60, 91, 96, 102, 103, 104, 110, 114, 128, 131, 132, 139, 141, 145, 157, 158, 159

family system/family therapy, 4, 14, 28, 29, 64, 73, 79, 91, 92, 96, 102, 114, 118, 133, 136, 139, 141, 149, 157, 164, 180, 183
fluidity of movement, 5, 98, 140
flow chart, step-by-step, 61
forming a group, 110–116
forming a relationship, *x*, 18, 19–26, 54, 55, 61, 64–67, 89, 138, 151–152, 157
freedom, *xi*, *xviii*, 5, 8, 26, 38, 44, 75, 97, 119, 155
frequency, length, and duration of groups, 110, 116–117
friendship, *xvii*, 4, 61, 71, 77, 79, 80, 144

G

getting, 103, 145–146, 147, 154
getting along with oneself, 62, 78
goal disclosure, 42, 45, 61, 145, 154
goals, *x*, *xvii*, 7, 8, 12, 35, 54, 60, 63, 65, 69, 77, 78, 79, 82, 84, 89, 90, 96, 98, 99, 101, 102, 111, 120, 123, 124, 127, 151, 152, 153, 155, 164, 166, 169, 172, 177, 178
  immediate, *xviii*, 8, 42, 43, 44, 46, 96, 97, 103, 104, 108, 131, 135, 137, 138, 140–150, 151, 154, 157, 159
  long term, 12, 61, 96, 99, 127
good/bad/right/wrong, 155
group(s), *ix*, *x*, *xi*, *xv*, *xx*, 4, 5, 7,
  agreements, 19, 23, 26, 55, 59, 61, 66–67, 89, 117, 125–126, 151–152, 177
  and human living, 3, 4, 11, 60, 62, 96, 104, 121, 128, 129, 136, 137, 138, 139–140
  as a corrective agent, 5, 11, 105, 109, 123, 152, 155
  cohesion, 9, 65, 69, 102, 110, 112, 122, 124, 151, 163, 177
  coleadership of, 161, 163, 178–182
  composition, 110, 112–114, 129, 176
  diversity, 79, 102, 111, 113, 114, 180
  experience, *x*, *xix*, 14, 17, 19, 63, 66, 82, 97, 100, 111, 116, 122, 128, 129, 136, 161, 162, 163–173, 176, 178, 179, 182
  flow chart, step-by-step, 61
guidance, 135, 136–137, 149, 151, 157

interventions, *x–xi*, 10, 12, 13, 17, 21, 55, 59, 60, 68, 73, 89, 100, 105, 120, 121, 122, 137, 138, 143, 149, 154, 162, 176, 177
leader, role of, 117–125
members, selection of, 110–112, 129
observation, 31, 42, 116, 161, 163, 173, 174, 175, 178, 182
participation, 8–9, 10, 11, 27, 30, 100, 102, 108, 120, 124, 176
presence, 64–65, 95, 100, 118–119, 120, 130
problem solving, 14, 39, 59, 86–88, 90, 122, 177
process, *ix*, *x*, *xix*, 6, 9, 11, 12, 13, 18, 20, 21, 26, 29, 32, 37, 51, 55, 60, 62, 63, 65, 66, 73, 78, 80, 81, 82, 84, 88, 89, 95, 96, 97, 100, 101, 102, 106, 108, 110, 113, 114, 115, 116, 117, 118, 120, 121, 122, 124–125, 128, 129, 130, 136, 138, 152, 154, 161, 162, 163, 164, 173, 174, 175, 176, 177, 178, 179, 180, 182
psychotherapy, *ix*, *xv*, *xx*, 8, 12, 13, 14, 15, 56, 59, 60, 89, 91, 92, 103, 108, 113, 130, 136, 138, 158, 159, 183, 184
setting, 64, 66, 110, 115–116
size, 64, 110, 114–115
structure, *x*, 3, 11–13, 59–93, 101, 145, 176, 177
supervision, 161, 163, 176, 178–182
termination, 61, 89, 116–117
theory, *ix*, *x*, 59–92, 95–134, 135–160
therapy, *ix*, *x*, *xv*, *xix*, *xx*, *xxi*, 3, 6, 8, 10, 12, 13, 14, 59, 60, 62, 64, 75–77, 80, 89, 90, 95, 97–98, 101, 103, 108, 110, 112, 113, 114, 128, 163, 173, 176
group counseling, *ix*, *x*, *xv*, *xix*, *xx*, *xxi*, 3, 6, 7, 8, 9, 13, 14, 17, 18, 59, 60–61, 62, 64, 75, 76, 80, 89, 90, 95, 97, 100, 101, 103, 108, 110, 111, 112, 113, 114, 115, 119, 121, 128, 129, 130, 131, 132, 133, chapter 5, 163, 168, 173, 176, 182, 183
  as development of voice, 9,
  as experiential learning, 8–9
  as investing social situations with real meaning, 10
  as structural, 11–12

as support, 9–10
as values forming, 10–11

H

hermeneutics/hermeneutical beings, 7, 60, 97, 99,
heterogeneous, 111, 112, 113
holism, x, 98, 123–124
homogeneous, 111, 112, 113
humor, xix, 37, 62, 86, 95, 122–123, 127, 130, 142

I

Idaho Conference on Adlerian Psychology, xv–xvi, xix, 18
Individual Psychology, xx, 96, 98, 102, 127, 130, 132, 133, 159, 183
  Journal of, 14, 15, 90, 91, 92, 130, 131, 132, 133, 157, 158, 159, 183
inferiority feelings, 99, 128
insight, x, 34, 36, 47, 100, 105, 107, 128, 129, 177
interests, x, 119, 126
interpretations, x, xviii, 4, 20, 32, 34, 53, 54, 55, 60, 69, 71, 72, 73, 74, 75, 76, 78, 81, 82, 83, 85, 86, 97, 99, 102, 107, 108, 120, 121, 138, 143, 151, 153–154, 155, 156, 171
interventions, group, x–xi, 10, 12, 13, 17, 21, 55, 59, 60, 68, 73, 89, 100, 105, 120, 121, 122, 137, 138, 143, 149, 154, 162, 176, 177
interview, xix, 6, 61, 65, 178,
  objective, 59, 61, 68, 71–84, 90, 153
  subjective, 59, 61, 67–68, 69 70, 89, 152
intimacy, 62, 71, 77, 78, 79, 80, 178
ironclad logic of social living, 7
irrelevant, 164, 166, 167–168, 171

J

Journal for Specialists in Group Work, xix, xx, 56, 133, 184
Journal of Individual Psychology, 14, 15, 90, 91, 92, 130, 131, 132, 133, 157, 158, 159, 183
journals and journaling, 161, 173–175, 182

K

Kebb, story of, 155–156
kinkeeping, 62, 78, 79

L

leadership, x, xiii, xvii, 9, 11, 12, 17, 18, 20, 21, 22, 24, 26, 27, 31, 33, 34, 44, 45, 46, 48, 49, 50, 52, 54, 60, 64, 68, 69, 73, 82, 84, 88, 89, 95, 101, 103, 106, 107, 108, 109, 110, 115, 116, 117–125, 128, 129, 130, 138, 149, 151, 152, 161, 163, 164, 168, 173, 174, 175, 176, 177, 178–180
life tasks, 59, 61, 62, 70, 71, 77–80, 90, 91, 92, 176
lifestyle, lifestyle assessment, x, xviii, 71, 82, 91, 92, 97, 99, 102, 128, 138, 153, 158, 159, 163, 176, 184
lighting, 64, 115
logistics, 64, 95, 110–117

M

meaning, ix, x, xviii, xix, 36, 60, 63, 68, 79, 81, 82, 86, 89, 90, 107, 122, 125, 165, 166, 171, 173, 174, 176
  personal, 3, 10, 54, 60, 68, 69, 72, 75, 78, 79, 81, 82, 84, 128, 129, 177
  interactive, 3, 8, 10, 14, 44, 54, 103, 104, 105, 120, 129, 151, 180
meeting group members, 59, 65–66, 89
mistakes, xviii, 8, 47, 50, 54, 70, 81, 97, 100, 102, 111, 137, 180
mistaken goals of children's
misbehavior, 103, 108, 135, 138, 141–147, 151, 153, 154, 155, 157
mistaken notions of adults with children, 135, 137, 138, 142, 147–150, 157
modeling, 95, 101, 122, 124, 130, 176, 177
movement, fluidity of, 5, 98, 140
mutual respect, 4, 12, 64, 86, 88, 101, 107, 129, 151, 176

N

narratives, Narrative therapy, 7, 15, 63, 68, 72, 73, 155

Subject Index

National Association of Social Workers (NASW), 162
neurosis, neurotic behavior, 6, 14, 62, 80, 91, 127, 130, 183
new possibilities, 55, 59, 61, 86, 88, 90, 125, 129, 176, 178
nonconscious, 99, 105, 108, 145
noise, 64, 115

O

objective interview, 59, 61, 68, 71–84, 90, 153
occupation and work, 62, 71, 77, 78

P

parent "C" group, 70, 106, 110
parent study groups, 110, 128
patterns, 32, 40, 42, 43, 44, 49, 54, 59, 61, 64, 67, 68, 69, 70, 77, 81, 90, 95, 97, 98, 99, 100, 101, 103, 104, 105, 107, 112, 120, 122, 123, 124, 128, 130, 135, 137, 140, 141, 147, 151, 153, 157
perceptions, x, 68, 100, 104, 114, 133
perfection, xviii, 89, 96, 99, 123, 134
personality priorities, 161, 163–174
personal meaning, 3, 10, 54, 60, 68, 69, 72, 75, 78, 79, 81, 82, 84, 128, 129, 177
placating, 164, 165, 166, 171
place, having a, xviii, 4, 5, 6–7, 10, 47, 49, 53, 73, 76, 79, 87, 88, 90, 109, 127, 140, 142, 151
   in the family, 4, 33, 73, 86, 136
   in the group, 4, 10, 65, 90, 99, 109, 117, 121, 129, 177
play therapy, 153, 159
pleasing, 164, 165, 166
postmodern, 7
power, power struggle, 29, 40, 41–43, 48–49, 53, 74, 87–88, 103, 41, 142, 143, 144, 145, 146, 147, 148, 149, 151, 154, 165
presence, 64–65, 95, 100, 118–119, 120, 130
private logic, 7, 99, 101, 140, 153
problem solving, group, 14, 39, 59, 86–88, 90, 122, 177

psychological disclosure, 6, 12, 18, 41–47, 54, 55, 59, 60, 61, 84–86, 89, 100, 104–108, 121, 128, 157
psychological hypothesis, 20, 23, 31–32, 55, 63, 72, 107, 108, 120, 142, 154
psychological investigation, 18, 26–41, 54, 55, 59, 60, 67–84, 89, 100, 145, 151, 152–153, 157, 176
psychological retreat, 6, 8, 62, 70, 78, 80, 140
psychological tolerance, 80
puppets, 153
purposes, xvii, xix, 7, 12, 31, 35, 36, 40, 41, 43, 44, 54, 59, 61, 62, 63, 64, 69, 70, 80, 81, 84, 89, 90, 98, 101, 102, 104, 108, 114, 123, 124, 129, 140, 141–147, 148, 153, 164, 177

Q

"The Question," x, 59, 61, 68, 70–71, 90, 102

R

rationale for Adlerian group work, 3–16
recognition reflex, xvii, 42, 44, 59, 103, 145, 147, 154, 159
reeducation, x, 86–89, 100, 108–110, 138
relationship, forming a, x, 18, 19–26, 54, 55, 61, 64–67, 89, 138, 151–152, 157
reorientation, x, 6, 12, 47–54, 55, 59, 60, 61, 86–89, 96, 97, 100, 101, 108–110, 14, 151, 153, 155–156, 157, 177
revenge, 103, 141, 142, 143, 144, 145, 147, 148, 154
risk(s), 20. 54, 62, 86, 95, 107, 108, 119–121, 130
role of group leader, 117–125
role playing, 88, 91, 109, 153
role reversal, 153

S

safe emergency, 90
schools, counseling in, ix, xvi, 6, 11, 13, 26, 40, 60, 108–109, 110, 113–114, 115, 116, 117, 121, 136, 137, 139, 142, 146, 148, 149–150, 151, 162, 180

self–absorption, *xviii*, 80, 86, 99, 126
self–actualization, *xviii*, 89, 96, 99, 123, 134
self–disclosure, 128, 177
self–elevation, 100, 103, 104, 145, 146, 147, 154
self–esteem, 64, 90, 98, 123, 165
setting, group, 64, 66, 110, 115–116
significance, 164, 165, 166, 167, 169, 171
size, 64, 110, 114–115
social equality, 5, 7, 8, 10, 15, 52, 56, 80, 91, 101, 129, 132, 136, 158
social interest, *x*, *xviii*, *xix*, 7, 10, 62, 79, 80, 86, 90, 95, 99, 101, 118, 126, 127–128, 130, 151, 157, 163, 171, 172, 173, 183
Sonstegard's life and work, *xv–xx*, 17–56, 181–182
STEP, 13, 14, 110, 114, 131, 158
Step-by-step, 60
group counseling and therapy, 17–56, 57–93
 group flow chart, 61, 89
strengths and weaknesses, 63, 152
striving, *x*, *xviii*, 19, 99, 127
strong/weak, 7
style of living, *x*, *xviii*, 71, 82, 91, 92, 97, 99, 102, 128, 138, 153, 158, 159, 163, 176, 184
subjective approach to psychology, *x*
subjective interview, 59, 61, 67–68, 69–70, 89, 152
superiority, *xviii*, 5, 7, 45, 46, 47, 90, 99, 127, 131, 164, 165, 166, 169
super reasonable, 164, 166, 167, 170
support, 3, 4, 9–10, 12, 14, 59, 61, 63, 77, 79, 80, 88, 89, 90, 105, 112, 113, 124, 163, 170, 177

systemic orientation, *xviii*, 5, 6, 7, 8, 10, 11, 12, 14, 31, 60, 62, 71, 73, 96, 102, 108, 111, 121, 123, 139, 142, 146, 163

T

tasks of life, 59, 61, 62, 70, 71, 77–80, 90, 91, 92, 176
teleology, *x*, 7, 13, 60, 95, 96, 97, 98, 102, 107, 120, 122, 123, 124, 127, 128, 130, 145
tentative disclosures, 12, 73, 85, 107, 120, 145, 151, 128,154
terminating an interview, 61, 89, 116–117
training of group leaders, chapter 6
typescript of group counseling session, 19–54

U

unconscious, 99, 105, 108, 145

V

values, clarification and formation, *x*, 3, 10–11, 14, 52, 84, 100, 117, 128, 129, 148, 149
Vienna, *ix*, 6, 60, 96
voice, development of, 3, 9, 10, 14, 15, 18, 51, 55, 65–66, 101, 113, 132, 136, 163, 176, 183

Made in the USA
Lexington, KY
11 July 2019